GRANDMA'S BEST RECIPES

Love Food ® is an imprint of Parragon Books Ltd

Parragon
Queen Street House
4 Queen Street
Bath BA1 1HE, UK

Copyright © Parragon Books Ltd 2007

Love Food ® and the accompanying heart device is a trade mark of Parragon Books Ltd

ISBN 978-1-4075-0429-2

Internal design by Jane Bozzard-Hill
Cover design by Emily Lewis
Photography by Clive Bozzard-Hill
Home economists: Sandra Baddeley and Valerie Barrett
Introduction by Pamela Gwyther

Printed in China

Notes for the reader
This book uses metric and imperial measurements. Follow the same units of measurement
throughout; do not mix metric and imperial. All spoon measurements are level, unless
otherwise stated; teaspoons are assumed to be 5 ml, and tablespoons are assumed to be
15 ml. Unless otherwise stated, milk is assumed to be whole, eggs and individual fruits,
such as bananas, are medium, and pepper is freshly ground black pepper.

Recipes using raw or lightly cooked eggs should be avoided by infants, the elderly,
pregnant women, convalescents and anyone suffering from an illness. Pregnant and
breast-feeding women are advised to avoid eating peanuts and peanut products.

GRANDMA'S BEST RECIPES

$\mathcal{C}$ONTENTS

$\mathcal{I}$NTRODUCTION

This is a book about all of our favourite childhood food memories, and it will give you the opportunity to create dishes 'just like Grandma used to make'. It will conjure up all the wonderful food smells that would always be present when we went to visit our grandparents as children, and the warm home-cooked meals that were waiting for us. It would be particularly welcoming to arrive when Grandma had just been baking and there was a selection of cakes and biscuits, and even freshly baked bread to smother with butter and eat fresh from the oven. Grandma's food was always a comfort; just the right thing to cheer you up, soothe a cold or even help heal a broken heart. Like Grandma herself, her food was always there and could be relied upon in all circumstances.

'Grandma's food was always a comfort – just the thing to cheer you up'

For many of us, our childhoods were very much linked to our grandparents. When we visited them for Christmas and other holidays, all the traditional foods would appear as if by magic. It is only with hindsight that we appreciate the amount of planning and hard work that went into making our perfect holidays. Often we would not only be able to eat the food but also have the thrill of helping to make it. Somehow, Grandma always had time to allow us to roll out the pastry and biscuits and help mix the cakes. She even allowed us to lick the wooden spoon and scrape the mixing bowl to try the delicious mix before it went in the oven. It was here that many of us learned to cook as Grandma was able to spend time with us and pass on the considerable knowledge that she had acquired over the years.

Weekends spent at our grandparents' often meant a traditional roast would be served. In addition to a huge joint of meat, there would be all the accompaniments: the vegetables, roast potatoes and parsnips, oodles of gravy and always Yorkshire pudding, even when it wasn't beef. The meal would always be followed by a wonderful pudding – apple pie, rhubarb crumble or maybe a lemon meringue pie. When there was a celebration, like a birthday, there might even be a Black Forest gateau or an iced cake with candles for the birthday girl or boy to blow out.

The food Grandma prepared for everyday meals was simpler. Firstly, because times were harder in her day, the maximum use was made of leftovers, such as shepherd's pie and bubble and squeak using the remnants from the Sunday roast. Meals tended to be rather heavy as people often had to do more physical work and didn't have cars, so would walk relatively long distances. Casseroles and stews using the cheaper cuts of meat were prepared and cooked for a long time in a slow oven so that the meat would be really tender. Sausages and potatoes were also popular as they were filling and economical. Vegetables were often home-grown so they were fresh and in season. Some of the surplus vegetable and fruits would be preserved for use later in the year – fruit was turned into jam and vegetables were salted or made into chutneys.

Today's generation of grandmothers is more likely to be engaged full-time in the workplace and trying to juggle home, family, work, hobbies, interests and travels abroad. Her time for cooking has been reduced and she probably saves the traditional foods for special occasions and chooses quicker and healthier recipes in her day-to-day cooking. Her food habits are changing too, influenced by travel to far-away places and sampling the local fare. Today's multicultural society also means

'Like Grandma herself, her food could be relied upon
in all circumstances'

that we eat different foods on different occasions and celebrate new festivals. We also have a wider variety of food ingredients available, making many exciting new recipes and exotic meals far more accessible.

As the years have passed, our eating habits have changed. Foods that would have been considered exotic twenty years ago have become part of our everyday life – and comfort foods in their own right. Chicken tikka masala has overtaken roast beef as our nation's favourite dish. Pizza is another example of a food which has been absorbed into our national food identity along with others, such as chicken Kiev, spaghetti Bolognese and chilli con carne. This is a result of the changing population of our own country and the fact that many of us now have the opportunity to travel throughout the world. Most of our grandparents did not get the chance to journey much further than their own backyards, but global travel has widened the range of food experiences for today's generation. South American, Asian and Eastern European foods have all become part of our regular diet in recent years.

The way we eat has also changed through recent years. Although many will say that it is a shame that families tend not to sit down together for meals anymore, some food habits have changed for the better. We eat a lighter diet and consume more good-quality fresh fruits and vegetables now that these are available throughout the year. We are much more aware of what foods are good for us, although our busy lifestyles often lead us to make unwise food choices and to give in to the convenience of ready-made food or takeaways.

Obviously at the weekends, when we have more time, the favourite recipes come into their own. Although they may have a newer twist or include a prepared ingredient, like ready-to-use pastry, they are essentially the foods we ate in our childhood. Also, when there is a birthday or anniversary we tend to make more of an effort in preparing the food and are more extravagant with its selection. This is also the time when we might bake, providing family or friends with something delicious, like gingerbread or coffee and walnut cake, to accompany a cup of tea or coffee. Some people spend some of their time at weekends preparing home-cooked food and then freezing it for later in the week. In order to do this you need to be organised and have large saucepans so that you can make dishes in large quantities, but it is worth the effort.

Comfort foods are the old favourites: the meals that are particularly familiar to us, give us a warm feeling and soothe our souls. Grandma made these for us when we were young, so the good feelings associated with them are still there. When we are upset, worried or depressed, simple food like a warming chicken or tomato soup is just what is needed. Dishes that you can eat with your hands, such as a grilled cheese sandwich or a tasty hamburger, are just the thing when you don't feel like sitting at the table with a

GRANDMA'S COMFORT FOOD

knife and fork. A casserole is an excellent standby for a cold winter's day and provides a great opportunity to get the family sitting around the table, eating and discussing the day's occurrences. Other familiar foods, like traditional roast chicken, fish pie and baked potatoes, are all covered in this chapter so, whenever you need them, you'll have heartening recipes to hand, just like the ones your Grandma might have cooked for you.

TOMATO SOUP

SERVES 4
55 g/2 oz butter
I onion, finely chopped
700 g/I lb 9 oz tomatoes, finely chopped
salt and pepper
600 ml/I pint hot chicken or
  vegetable stock

pinch of sugar
2 tbsp shredded fresh basil leaves, plus
  extra sprigs to garnish
I tbsp chopped fresh parsley
croûtons, to serve (optional)

GRANDMA'S TIPS
When fresh tomatoes are out of season and tasteless, use 800 g/ 1 lb 12 oz canned tomatoes. Using canned tomatoes will not only give your soup some extra sweetness, but will also save you time. For a special treat and for extra warmth in the winter, add a tablespoon of sherry to each bowl before serving.

1 Melt half the butter in a large, heavy-based saucepan. Add the onion and cook over a low heat, stirring occasionally, for 5 minutes, or until softened. Add the tomatoes, season to taste with salt and pepper and cook for 5 minutes.

2 Pour in the hot chicken or vegetable stock, return to the boil, then reduce the heat and cook for 10 minutes.

3 Push the soup through a sieve with the back of a wooden spoon to remove the tomato skins and seeds. Return to the saucepan and stir in the sugar, remaining butter, basil and parsley. Heat through briefly, but do not allow to boil. Ladle into warmed serving bowls. Serve immediately, garnished with sprigs of basil and accompanied by croûtons, if you wish.

CREAM OF CHICKEN SOUP

SERVES 4
3 tbsp butter
4 shallots, chopped
1 leek, trimmed and sliced
450 g/1 lb skinless chicken breasts,
  chopped
600 ml/1 pint chicken stock

1 tbsp chopped fresh parsley
1 tbsp chopped fresh thyme
salt and pepper
175 ml/6 fl oz double cream
sprigs of fresh thyme, to garnish
fresh crusty rolls, to serve

GRANDMA'S TIPS

If you have just cooked a whole chicken for a meal, you can make a stock with the leftovers. Place the carcass in a large saucepan of water along with a chopped onion, carrot and celery stick. Bring to the boil, then simmer for 1–1¼ hours. Strain and carefully remove any meat from the bones and set aside. Make the soup according to the recipe, adding the cooked chicken pieces either before blending or just before serving.

1 Melt the butter in a large saucepan over a medium heat. Add the shallots and cook, stirring, for 3 minutes, until slightly softened. Add the leek and cook for a further 5 minutes, stirring. Add the chicken, stock and herbs, and season with salt and pepper. Bring to the boil, then lower the heat and simmer for 25 minutes, until the chicken is tender and cooked through. Remove from the heat and leave to cool for 10 minutes.

2 Transfer the soup into a food processor and blend until smooth (you may need to do this in batches). Return the soup to the pan and warm over a low heat for 5 minutes.

3 Stir in the cream and cook for a further 2 minutes, then remove from the heat and ladle into serving bowls. Garnish with sprigs of thyme and serve with fresh crusty rolls.

GRILLED CHEESE
SANDWICH

SERVES 2
100 g/3½ oz Gruyère or Emmental
    cheese, grated
4 slices white bread, with the crusts
    trimmed
2 thick slices ham
1 small egg, beaten
3 tbsp unsalted butter, plus extra if
    necessary

for the white sauce
2 tbsp unsalted butter
1 tsp sunflower oil
½ tbsp plain flour
125 ml/4 fl oz warm milk
pepper

1 Spread half the cheese on 2 bread slices, then top each with a slice of ham, cut to fit. Sprinkle the ham with all but 2 tablespoons of the remaining cheese, then sandwich together with the remaining bread slices and press down well.

2 To make the sauce, melt the butter with the oil in a small, heavy-based pan and stir in the flour until well combined and smooth. Cook over a medium heat, stirring constantly, for 1 minute. Remove from the heat and stir in a little of the milk until well incorporated. Return to the heat and gradually add the remaining milk, stirring constantly, until it has all been incorporated. Cook for a further 3 minutes, or until the sauce is smooth and thickened. Stir in the remaining cheese and pepper to taste, then set aside and keep warm.

3 Beat the egg in a shallow dish. Add 1 sandwich and press down to coat on both sides, then remove from the dish and repeat with the other sandwich.

4 Preheat the grill to high. Line a baking tray with foil and set aside. Melt the butter in a sauté pan or frying pan and cook 1 or both sandwiches, depending on the size of your pan, over a medium-high heat until golden brown on both sides. Add a little extra butter, if necessary, if you have to cook the sandwiches separately.

5 Transfer the sandwiches to the foil-lined baking tray and spread the white sauce over the top. Cook under the grill, about 10 cm/4 inches from the heat, for 4 minutes, or until golden and brown.

BACON BUTTIES

SERVES 1
2 smoked bacon rashers
15 g/½ oz butter, softened
2 slices thick white or brown bread

pepper
1 tomato, sliced (optional)
sauce of choice (brown sauce, tomato
ketchup or mustard)

GRANDMA'S TIPS

*These traditional 'door-step'
butties can be made using thinly
sliced bread with the addition of
lettuce to make a BLT (bacon,
lettuce and tomato) – the sauce
is optional. For an even more
exotic sarnie, add some slices of
avocado.*

1 Cut the rashers of bacon in half so that you have 2 pieces of back bacon and 2 pieces of streaky.

2 Place the bacon under a hot grill and grill, turning frequently, until the bacon is cooked and as crispy as you like it.

3 Meanwhile, butter the bread.

4 Place 2 pieces of bacon on one slice of bread and season with a grinding of pepper. Add the tomato, if using, and the sauce. Top with the remaining bacon and the other slice of bread and eat immediately.

ROAST CHICKEN

SERVES 6
1 free-range chicken, weighing 2.25 kg/
    5 lb
55 g/2 oz butter
2 tbsp chopped fresh lemon thyme

salt and pepper
1 lemon, quartered
125 ml/4 fl oz white wine
6 fresh thyme sprigs, to garnish

GRANDMA'S TIPS

This is the quintessential roast chicken recipe. If you want even more flavour to the bird, stuff it with a finely chopped onion, the grated rind and juice of 1 lemon and some fresh thyme leaves mixed with a few soft breadcrumbs. For an even more robust variation, stuff the bird with 40 cloves of garlic – it will be delicious and milder than you might think, as the cooking renders the garlic sweet and not so pungent.

1 Preheat the oven to 220°C/425°F/Gas Mark 7. Make sure the chicken is clean, wiping it inside and out using kitchen paper, and place in a roasting tin.

2 Place the butter in a bowl and soften with a fork, then mix in the thyme and season well with salt and pepper. Butter the chicken all over with the herb butter, inside and out, and place the lemon quarters inside the body cavity. Pour the wine over the chicken.

3 Roast the chicken in the centre of the oven for 20 minutes. Reduce the temperature to 190°C/375°F/Gas Mark 5 and continue to roast for a further 1¼ hours, basting frequently. Cover with foil if the skin begins to brown too much. If the tin dries out, add a little more wine or water.

4 Test that the chicken is cooked by piercing the thickest part of the leg with a sharp knife or skewer and making sure the juices run clear. Remove from the oven.

5 Remove the chicken from the roasting tin and place on a warmed serving plate to rest, covered with foil, for 10 minutes before carving.

6 Place the roasting tin on the top of the hob and bubble the pan juices gently over a low heat until they have reduced and are thick and glossy. Season to taste with salt and pepper.

7 Serve the chicken with the pan juices and scatter with the thyme sprigs.

POTATO, LEEK & CHICKEN PIE

SERVES 4

225 g/8 oz waxy potatoes, cubed
5 tbsp butter
1 skinless chicken breast fillet, about
    175 g/6 oz, cubed
1 leek, sliced
150 g/5½ oz chestnut mushrooms, sliced

2½ tbsp plain flour
300 ml/10 fl oz milk
1 tbsp Dijon mustard
2 tbsp chopped fresh sage
225 g/8 oz filo pastry, thawed if frozen
3 tbsp butter, melted
salt and pepper

1 Preheat the oven to 180°C/350°F/Gas Mark 4. Cook the potato cubes in a saucepan of boiling water for 5 minutes. Drain and set aside.

2 Melt the butter in a frying pan and cook the chicken cubes for 5 minutes or until browned all over.

3 Add the leek and mushrooms and cook for 3 minutes, stirring. Stir in the flour and cook for 1 minute stirring constantly. Gradually stir in the milk and bring to the boil. Add the mustard, sage and potato cubes, season to taste with salt and pepper and simmer for 10 minutes.

4 Meanwhile, line a deep pie dish with half of the sheets of filo pastry. Spoon the sauce into the dish and cover with 1 sheet of pastry. Brush the pastry with butter and lay another sheet on top. Brush this sheet with butter.

5 Cut the remaining filo pastry into strips and fold them on to the top of the pie to create a ruffled effect. Brush the strips with the melted butter and cook in the preheated oven for 45 minutes or until golden brown and crisp. Serve hot.

ROAST BEEF

SERVES 8

1 prime rib of beef joint, weighing
   2.7 kg/6 lb
salt and pepper
2 tsp dry English mustard

3 tbsp plain flour
300 ml/10 fl oz red wine
300 ml/10 fl oz beef stock
2 tsp Worcestershire sauce (optional)
Yorkshire pudding, to serve

GRANDMA'S TIPS

Instead of making a traditional gravy, you can just pour off the fat and add enough red wine to deglaze the pan. Season to taste and serve immediately. This is known as a 'jus'.

1 Preheat the oven to 230°C/450°F/Gas Mark 8.

2 Season the meat to taste with salt and pepper. Rub in the mustard and 1 tablespoon of the flour.

3 Place the meat in a roasting tin large enough to hold it comfortably and roast in the oven for 15 minutes. Reduce the temperature to 190°C/375°F/Gas Mark 5 and cook for 15 minutes per 450 g/1 lb, plus 15 minutes (1¾ hours for this joint) for rare beef or 20 minutes per 450 g/1 lb, plus 20 minutes (2 hours 20 minutes) for medium beef. Baste the meat from time to time to keep it moist, and if the tin becomes too dry, add a little stock or red wine.

4 Remove the meat from the oven and place on a warmed serving plate, cover with foil and leave in a warm place for 10–15 minutes.

5 To make the gravy, pour off most of the fat from the tin, leaving behind the meat juices and the sediment. Place the tin on the hob over a medium heat and scrape all the sediment from the base of the tin. Sprinkle in the remaining flour and quickly mix it into the juices with a small whisk. When you have a smooth paste, gradually add the wine and most of the stock, whisking constantly. Bring to the boil, then reduce the heat to a gentle simmer and cook for 2–3 minutes. Season to taste with salt and pepper and add the remaining stock, if needed, and a little Worcestershire sauce, if you like.

6 When ready to serve, carve the meat into slices and serve on warmed plates. Pour the gravy into a warmed jug and take direct to the table. Serve with Yorkshire pudding.

BEEF STEW WITH
HERB DUMPLINGS

SERVES 6
3 tbsp olive oil
2 onions, finely sliced
2 garlic cloves, chopped
1 kg/2 lb 4 oz good-quality braising steak
2 tbsp plain flour
salt and pepper
300 ml/10 fl oz beef stock
bouquet garni
150 ml/5 fl oz red wine
1 tbsp chopped fresh parsley, to garnish

for the herb dumplings
115 g/4 oz self-raising flour, plus extra
   for shaping
55 g/2 oz suet or vegetable shortening
1 tsp mustard
1 tbsp chopped fresh parsley
1 tsp chopped fresh sage
salt and pepper
4 tbsp cold water

GRANDMA'S TIPS

You can make the stew the day before and refrigerate it overnight. Reheat 20 minutes before you're ready to add the dumplings, and proceed with the recipe. This will enhance the flavour of the stew and makes for fresh and light dumplings. You can vary the herbs used — try rosemary or thyme — and add some crushed garlic if you like.

1 Preheat the oven to 150°C/300°F/Gas Mark 2.

2 Heat 1 tablespoon of the oil in a large frying pan and fry the onion and garlic until soft and brown. Remove from the pan using a slotted spoon and place in a large casserole dish.

3 Trim the meat and cut into thick strips. Using the remaining oil, fry the meat in the frying pan over a high heat, stirring well until it is brown all over.

4 Sprinkle in the flour and stir well to prevent lumps. Season well with salt and pepper.

5 Over a medium heat, pour in the stock, stirring all the time to make a smooth sauce, then continue to heat until boiling.

6 Carefully turn the contents of the frying pan into the casserole dish. Add the bouquet garni and the wine. Cover and cook gently for 2–2½ hours.

7 Start making the dumplings 20 minutes before the stew is ready. Place the flour, suet, mustard, parsley, sage, and salt and pepper to taste in a bowl and mix well. Just before adding the dumplings to the stew, add enough of the water to the mixture to form a firm but soft dough. Break the dough into 12 pieces and roll them into round dumplings (you might need some flour on your hands for this).

8 Remove the stew from the oven, check the seasoning, discard the bouquet garni and add the dumplings, pushing them down under the liquid. Cover and return the dish to the oven, continuing to cook for 15 minutes until the dumplings have doubled in size.

9 Serve piping hot with the parsley scattered over the top.

STEAK & KIDNEY PIE

SERVES 4–6

butter, for greasing
700 g/1 lb 9 oz braising steak, trimmed
  and cut into 4-cm/1½-inch pieces
3 lambs' kidneys, cored and cut into
  2.5-cm/1-inch pieces
2 tbsp plain flour, plus extra for dusting
salt and pepper

3 tbsp vegetable oil
1 onion, roughly chopped
1 garlic clove, finely chopped
125 ml/4 fl oz red wine
450 ml/16 fl oz stock
1 bay leaf
400 g/14 oz ready-made puff pastry
1 egg, beaten

1 Preheat the oven to 160°C/325°F/Gas Mark 3. Grease a 1.2-litre/2-pint pie dish.

2 Put the prepared meat with the flour and salt and pepper in a large plastic bag and shake until all the meat is well coated.

3 Heat the oil in a flameproof casserole over a high heat and brown the meat in batches. Remove from the casserole with a slotted spoon and keep warm. Fry the onion and garlic in the casserole for 2–3 minutes until softening.

4 Stir in the wine and scrape the base of the pan to release the sediment. Pour in the stock, stirring constantly, and bring to the boil. Bubble for 2–3 minutes. Add the bay leaf and return the meat to the casserole. Cover and cook in the centre of the oven for 1½–2 hours. Check the seasoning, then remove the bay leaf. Leave the meat to cool, preferably overnight, to develop the flavours.

5 Preheat the oven to 200°C/400°F/Gas Mark 6.

6 Roll out the pastry on a lightly floured work surface to about 7 cm/2¾ inches larger than the pie dish. Cut off a 3-cm/1¼-inch strip from the edge. Moisten the rim of the dish and press the pastry strip onto it. Place the pie funnel in the centre of the dish and spoon in the steak and kidney filling. Don't overfill, keeping any extra gravy to serve separately. Moisten the pastry collar with water and put on the pastry lid, taking care to fit it carefully around the pie funnel. Crimp the edges of the pastry firmly and glaze with the egg.

7 Place the pie on a tray towards the top of the oven for about 30 minutes. The pie should be golden brown and the filling bubbling hot; cover it with foil and reduce the temperature if the pastry is getting too brown.

HAMBURGERS

SERVES 4–6
450 g/1 lb rump steak or topside,
    freshly minced
1 onion, grated
2–4 garlic cloves, crushed
2 tsp wholegrain mustard
pepper
2 tbsp olive oil

450 g/1 lb onions, finely sliced
2 tsp light muscovado sugar

to serve
4–6 sesame seed buns
lettuce
ketchup (optional)

1 Place the minced steak, grated onion, garlic, mustard and pepper in a large bowl and mix together. Shape into 4–6 equal-sized burgers, then cover and leave to chill for 30 minutes.

2 Meanwhile, heat the oil in a heavy-based frying pan. Add the onions and cook over a low heat for 10–15 minutes, or until the onions have caramelized. Add the sugar after 8 minutes and stir occasionally during cooking. Drain well on kitchen paper and keep warm.

3 Wipe the frying pan clean, then heat until hot. When hot, add the burgers and cook for 3–5 minutes on each side or until cooked to personal preference. Serve in sesame seed buns with the onions, lettuce and ketchup, if you like.

SHEPHERD'S PIE

SERVES 6
1 tbsp olive oil
2 onions, finely chopped
2 garlic cloves, finely chopped
675 g/1 lb 8 oz good-quality lamb mince
2 carrots, finely chopped
salt and pepper
1 tbsp plain flour
225 ml/8 fl oz beef or chicken stock
125 ml/4 fl oz red wine
Worcestershire sauce (optional)

for the mashed potato
675g g/1 lb 8 oz floury potatoes, such as
    King Edwards, Maris Piper or Desirée,
    peeled and cut into even-sized chunks
55 g/2 oz butter
2 tbsp cream or milk
salt and pepper

GRANDMA'S TIPS

To make a cottage pie, use minced beef instead of the lamb. Instead of the basic mashed potato topping, you could try using a mixture of mashed potatoes and carrot or parsnip. Alternatively, substitute grated potato for the mashed potatoes for a 'rösti-style' topping.

1 Preheat the oven to 180°C/350°F/Gas Mark 4.

2 Heat the oil in a large, flameproof casserole dish and fry the onion until softened, then add the garlic and stir well.

3 Raise the heat and add the meat. Cook quickly to brown the meat all over, stirring continually. Add the carrots and season well with salt and pepper.

4 Stir in the flour and add the stock and wine. Stir well and heat until simmering and thickened.

5 Cover the casserole dish and cook in the oven for about 1 hour. Check the consistency from time to time and add a little more stock or wine if required. The meat mixture should be quite thick but not dry. Season with salt and pepper to taste and add a little Worcestershire sauce, if desired.

6 While the meat is cooking, make the mashed potato. Cook the potatoes in a large saucepan of boiling salted water for 15–20 minutes. Drain well and mash with a potato masher until smooth. Add the butter and cream and season well with salt and pepper.

7 Spoon the lamb mixture into an ovenproof serving dish and spread or pipe the potato on top.

8 Increase the oven temperature to 200°C/400°F/Gas Mark 6 and cook the pie for 15–20 minutes at the top of the oven until golden brown. You might like to finish it off under a medium grill for a really crisp brown topping to the potato.

LAMB SHANKS WITH CANNELLINI BEANS

SERVES 4

250 g/9 oz cannellini beans, soaked
    overnight
2 tbsp sunflower oil
1 large onion, thinly sliced
4 carrots, chopped
2 celery sticks, thinly sliced
1 garlic clove, chopped

4 large lamb shanks
400 g/14 oz canned chopped tomatoes
300 ml/10 fl oz red wine
finely pared zest and juice of 1 orange
2 bay leaves
3 rosemary sprigs
225 ml/8 fl oz water
salt and pepper

1 Preheat the oven to 160°C/325°F/Gas Mark 3. Drain the soaked beans and rinse under cold running water. Put in a large pan of cold water, bring to the boil and skim off any scum, then boil rapidly for 10 minutes. Drain and set aside.

2 Meanwhile, heat the oil in a large, flameproof casserole, add the onion, and cook for 5 minutes, or until softened. Add the carrots and celery and cook for a further 5 minutes, or until beginning to soften and the onion is beginning to brown. Add the garlic and cook for a further 1 minute. Push the vegetables to the sides of the pan.

3 Add the lamb shanks to the pan and cook for about 5 minutes, until browned on all sides. Add the beans to the pan with the tomatoes, wine and orange zest and juice, and stir together. Add the bay leaves and rosemary. Pour in the water so that the liquid comes halfway up the shanks. Season with pepper but do not add salt as this will stop the beans from softening.

4 Bring to the boil, then cover the pan and cook in the oven for about 1 hour. Turn the shanks over in the stock then continue cooking for 1½ hours until the lamb and beans are tender. Remove the bay leaves, then taste and add salt and pepper if necessary. Serve hot.

TOAD IN THE HOLE

SERVES 4
oil, for greasing
115 g/4 oz plain flour
pinch of salt

1 egg, beaten
300 ml/10 fl oz milk
450 g/1 lb good-quality pork sausages
1 tbsp vegetable oil

GRANDMA'S TIPS

Try making toad in the hole with meat balls instead of sausages. Fried onion rings can also be added to the dish before adding the batter.

1 Grease a 20 x 25-cm/8 x 10-inch ovenproof dish or roasting tin.

2 Make the batter by sifting the flour and salt into a mixing bowl. Make a well in the centre and add the beaten egg and half the milk. Carefully stir the liquid into the flour until the mixture is smooth. Gradually beat in the remaining milk. Leave to stand for 30 minutes.

3 Preheat the oven to 220°C/425°F/Gas Mark 7.

4 Prick the sausages and place them in the dish. Sprinkle over the oil and cook the sausages in the oven for 10 minutes until they are beginning to colour and the fat has started to run and is sizzling.

5 Remove from the oven and quickly pour the batter over the sausages. Return to the oven and cook for 35–45 minutes until the batter is well risen and golden brown. Serve immediately.

FISH & CHIPS

SERVES 2
vegetable oil, for deep-frying
3 large potatoes, such as Cara or Desirée
2 thick cod or haddock fillets,
   175 g/6 oz each

salt and pepper
175 g/6 oz self-raising flour, plus extra
   for dusting
200 ml/7 fl oz cold lager
lemon wedges, to serve

1 Heat the oil in a temperature-controlled deep-fat fryer to 120°C/250°F, or in a heavy-based saucepan, checking the temperature with a thermometer, to blanch the chips. Preheat the oven to 150°C/300°F/Gas Mark 2.

2 Peel the potatoes and cut into even-sized chips. Fry for about 8–10 minutes, depending on size, until softened but not coloured. Remove from the oil, drain on kitchen paper and place in a warm dish in the warm oven. Increase the temperature of the oil to 180–190°C/350–375°F, or until a cube of bread browns in 30 seconds.

3 Meanwhile, season the fish with salt and pepper and dust it lightly with a little flour.

4 Make a thick batter by sieving the flour into a bowl with a little salt and whisking in most of the lager. Check the consistency before adding the remainder: it should be very thick, like double cream.

5 Dip one fillet into the batter and allow it to be thickly coated. Carefully place the fish in the hot oil, then repeat with the other fillet.

6 Cook for 8–10 minutes, depending on the thickness of the fish. Turn the fillets over halfway through the cooking time. Remove the fish from the fryer or saucepan, drain and keep warm.

7 Make sure the oil temperature is still at 180°C/350°F and return the chips to the fryer or saucepan. Cook for a further 2–3 minutes until golden brown and crispy. Drain and season with salt and pepper before serving with the battered fish and lemon wedges for squeezing over.

FISHERMAN'S PIE

SERVES 6
butter, for greasing
900 g/2 lb white fish fillets, such as
   plaice, skinned
salt and pepper
150 ml/5 fl oz dry white wine
1 tbsp chopped fresh parsley, tarragon
   or dill

175 g/6 oz small mushrooms, sliced
100 g/3½ oz butter
175 g/6 oz cooked peeled prawns
40 g/1½ oz plain flour
125 ml/4 fl oz double cream
900 g/2 lb floury potatoes, such as King
   Edwards, Maris Piper or Desirée,
   peeled and cut into even-sized chunks

1   Preheat the oven to 180°C/350°F/Gas Mark 4. Butter a 1.7-litre/3-pint baking dish.

2   Fold the fish fillets in half and place in the dish. Season well with salt and pepper, pour
over the wine and scatter over the herbs.

3   Cover with foil and bake for 15 minutes until the fish starts to flake. Strain off the
liquid and reserve for the sauce. Increase the oven temperature to 220°C/425°F/
Gas Mark 7.

4   Sauté the mushrooms in a frying pan with 15 g/½ oz of the butter and spoon over
the fish. Scatter over the prawns.

5   Heat 55 g/2 oz of the butter in a saucepan and stir in the flour. Cook for a few
minutes without browning, remove from the heat, then add the reserved cooking liquid
gradually, stirring well between each addition.

6   Return to the heat and gently bring to the boil, still stirring to ensure a smooth sauce.
Add the cream and season to taste with salt and pepper. Pour over the fish in the dish
and smooth over the surface.

7   Make the mashed potato by cooking the potatoes in boiling salted water for 15–20
minutes. Drain well and mash with a potato masher until smooth. Season to taste with
salt and pepper and add the remaining butter, stirring until melted.

8   Pile or pipe the potato onto the fish and sauce and bake for 10–15 minutes until
golden brown.

SALMON FISHCAKES

SERVES 4

700 g/1 lb 9 oz skinless salmon fillet,
  cut into cubes
300 ml/10 fl oz full-fat milk
1 bay leaf
100 g/3½ oz broccoli, steamed until
  tender
700 g/1 lb 9 oz potatoes, boiled and
  mashed

2 tbsp finely chopped fresh parsley
4 tbsp wholemeal plain flour
pepper
1 egg yolk
2 large eggs, beaten
150 g/5½ oz fresh wholemeal
  breadcrumbs
2 tbsp olive oil

GRANDMA'S TIPS

These absolutely delicious fishcakes can be made more economical by using canned salmon. The broccoli can be replaced with sautéed leeks or even some sweetcorn, which the kids will love. For a more sophisticated flavour, chopped dill can be used instead of the parsley and the fishcakes can be served with a dill sauce or mayonnaise.

1 Preheat the oven to 200°C/400°F/Gas Mark 6. Put the salmon in a saucepan with the milk and bay leaf and bring slowly up to a simmer. Simmer for 2 minutes, then remove the saucepan from the heat, lift out and discard the bay leaf and leave the fish in the milk to cool. When cooled, lift out the fish with a slotted spoon onto kitchen paper to drain.

2 Flake the fish into a large bowl. Put the broccoli in a food processor and pulse until smooth. Add to the fish with the mashed potatoes, parsley, 1 tablespoon of the flour, and pepper to taste. Add the egg yolk and mix well. If the mixture is a little dry, add some of the poaching milk; if too wet, add a little more flour.

3 Divide the mixture into 12 portions and shape each portion into a cake. Put the beaten eggs, remaining flour and the breadcrumbs on 3 separate plates. Roll each fishcake in the flour, then in the beaten egg, and then in the breadcrumbs to coat.

4 Heat the oil in a non-stick baking tray in the preheated oven for 5 minutes. Add the fishcakes and bake for 10 minutes, then carefully turn the fishcakes over and bake for a further 10 minutes. Serve hot.

WINTER VEGETABLE COBBLER

SERVES 4
1 tbsp olive oil
1 garlic clove, crushed
8 small onions, halved
2 celery sticks, sliced
225 g/8 oz swede, chopped
2 carrots, sliced
½ small head of cauliflower, broken into florets
225 g/8 oz button mushrooms, sliced
400 g/14 oz canned chopped tomatoes
55 g/2 oz red lentils, rinsed
2 tbsp cornflour
3–4 tbsp water

300 ml/10 fl oz vegetable stock
2 tsp Tabasco sauce
2 tsp chopped fresh oregano
fresh oregano sprigs, to garnish

for the topping
225 g/8 oz self-raising flour
pinch of salt
4 tbsp butter
115 g/4 oz grated mature Cheddar cheese
2 tsp chopped fresh oregano
1 egg, lightly beaten
150 ml/5 fl oz milk

GRANDMA'S TIPS

This rib-sticking dish is just the thing for those cold winter evenings. The vegetables can be varied according to taste and season. You might like to make a curry-flavoured cobbler by using curry paste instead of the Tabasco sauce. The topping can be made with wholemeal flour instead of white for a healthier version.

1 Preheat the oven to 180°C/350°F/Gas Mark 4. Heat the oil in a large frying pan and cook the garlic and onions over a low heat for 5 minutes. Add the celery, swede, carrots and cauliflower and cook for 2–3 minutes.

2 Add the mushrooms, tomatoes and lentils. Place the cornflour and water in a bowl and mix to make a smooth paste. Stir into the frying pan with the stock, Tabasco and oregano. Transfer to an ovenproof dish, cover and bake in the preheated oven for 20 minutes.

3 To make the topping, sift the flour and salt into a bowl. Add the butter and rub it in, then stir in most of the cheese and oregano. Beat the egg with the milk in a small bowl and add enough to the dry ingredients to make a soft dough. Knead, then roll out on a lightly floured work surface to 1 cm/½ inch thick. Cut into 5-cm/2-inch rounds.

4 Remove the dish from the oven and increase the temperature to 200°C/400°F/Gas Mark 6. Arrange the dough rounds around the edge of the dish, brush with the remaining egg and milk mixture and sprinkle with the reserved cheese. Cook for a further 10–12 minutes. Garnish with oregano sprigs and serve.

ROASTED BUTTERNUT SQUASH RISOTTO

SERVES 4

600 g/1 lb 5 oz butternut squash or
    pumpkin, peeled and cut into
    bite-sized pieces
4 tbsp olive oil
1 tsp clear honey
25 g/1 oz fresh basil, plus extra sprigs
    to garnish

25 g/1 oz fresh oregano
1 tbsp margarine
2 onions, finely chopped
450 g/1 lb arborio or other risotto rice
175 ml/6 fl oz dry white wine
1.2 litres/2 pints vegetable stock
salt and pepper

1 Preheat the oven to 200°C/400°F/Gas Mark 6. Put the squash into a roasting tin. Mix
1 tablespoon of the oil with the honey and spoon over the squash. Turn the squash to
coat it in the mixture. Roast in the preheated oven for 30–35 minutes, or until tender.

2 Meanwhile, put the basil and oregano into a food processor with 2 tablespoons of the
remaining oil and process until finely chopped and blended. Set aside.

3 Heat the margarine and remaining oil in a large, heavy-based saucepan over a medium
heat. Add the onions and fry, stirring occasionally, for 8 minutes, or until soft and
golden. Add the rice and cook for 2 minutes, stirring to coat the grains in the oil mixture.

4 Pour in the wine and bring to the boil. Reduce the heat slightly and cook until the wine
is almost absorbed. Add the stock, a little at a time, and cook over a medium-low heat,
stirring constantly, for 20 minutes.

5 Gently stir in the herb oil and squash until thoroughly mixed into the rice and cook
for a further 5 minutes, or until the rice is creamy and cooked but retaining a little bite in
the centre of the grain. Season well with salt and pepper before serving, garnished with
sprigs of basil.

MACARONI CHEESE

SERVES 4
600 ml/1 pint milk
1 onion, peeled
8 peppercorns
1 bay leaf
55 g/2 oz butter
40 g/1½ oz plain flour
½ tsp ground nutmeg

5 tbsp double cream
pepper
100 g/3½ oz mature Cheddar cheese, grated
100 g/3½ oz Roquefort cheese, crumbled
350 g/12 oz dried macaroni
100 g/3½ oz Gruyère or Emmental cheese, grated

1 Put the milk, onion, peppercorns and bay leaf in a pan and bring to the boil. Remove from the heat and let stand for 15 minutes.

2 Melt the butter in a pan and stir in the flour until well combined and smooth. Cook over a medium heat, stirring constantly, for 1 minute. Remove from the heat. Strain the milk to remove the solids and stir a little into the butter and flour mixture until well incorporated. Return to the heat and gradually add the remaining milk, stirring constantly, until it has all been incorporated. Cook for a further 3 minutes, or until the sauce is smooth and thickened, then add the nutmeg, cream and pepper to taste. Add the Cheddar and Roquefort cheeses and stir until melted.

3 Meanwhile, bring a large pan of water to the boil. Add the macaroni, then return to the boil and cook for 8–10 minutes, or until just tender. Drain well and add to the cheese sauce. Stir well together.

4 Preheat the grill to high. Spoon the mixture into an ovenproof serving dish, then scatter over the Gruyère cheese and cook under the grill until bubbling and brown.

SOUFFLÉD BAKED
POTATOES

SERVES 4
2 baking potatoes, scrubbed
1 tbsp olive oil
2 tbsp full-fat milk
25 g/1 oz butter
25 g/1 oz Cheddar or Gruyère cheese,
   grated

1 large egg, separated
salt and pepper
2 slices ham, cooked turkey or unsmoked
   bacon, chopped
2 tbsp finely grated Parmesan cheese
salad, to serve

GRANDMA'S TIPS
Baked potatoes make for the perfect meal, particularly when they are stuffed with lots of tasty ingredients such as Bolognese or chilli sauce, flaked fish or ratatouille. Make sure the potatoes are baked through so that they're soft inside and the skins are firm and crispy, which makes them most delicious. You can even rub salt into the skins with the oil to enhance the flavour.

1 Preheat the oven to 200°C/400°F/Gas Mark 6. Prick the potatoes with a fork. Rub the oil all over the potatoes, place on a baking sheet and bake in the preheated oven for 1 hour, or until the flesh is soft.

2 Remove the potatoes from the oven, cut in half lengthways and carefully scoop out the flesh into a bowl, keeping the skins intact. Set the skins aside.

3 Add the milk, butter, Cheddar cheese and egg yolk to the potato and mash well. Season to taste with salt and pepper. Mix in the ham.

4 In a separate, grease-free bowl, whisk the egg white until stiff, then fold into the potato mixture.

5 Pile the potato mixture back into the skins and sprinkle over the Parmesan cheese. Return to the oven and bake for 20 minutes. Serve with salad.

PERFECT MASH

SERVES 4

900 g/2 lb floury potatoes, such as King
   Edwards, Maris Piper or Desirée

4 tbsp butter
3 tbsp hot milk
salt and pepper

1 Peel the potatoes, placing them in cold water as you prepare the others to prevent them from going brown.

2 Cut the potatoes into even-sized chunks and cook in a large saucepan of boiling salted water over a medium heat, covered, for 20–25 minutes until they are tender. Test with the point of a knife, but make sure you test right in the middle to avoid lumps.

3 Remove the pan from the heat and drain the potatoes. Return the potatoes to the hot pan and mash with a potato masher until smooth.

4 Add the butter and continue to mash until it is all mixed in, then add the milk (it is better hot because the potatoes absorb it more quickly to produce a creamier mash).

5 Taste the mashed potatoes and season with salt and pepper as necessary. Serve at once.

CAULIFLOWER CHEESE

SERVES 4

1 cauliflower, trimmed and cut into florets
 (675 g/1 lb 8 oz prepared weight)
40 g/1½ oz butter
40 g/1½ oz plain flour

450 ml/16 fl oz milk
115 g/4 oz Cheddar cheese, finely grated
whole nutmeg, for grating
salt and pepper
1 tbsp grated Parmesan cheese

GRANDMA'S TIPS

Using a mixture of cauliflower and broccoli will give a more colourful dish. You can make it even more substantial by adding some fried sliced onions and fried bacon pieces before pouring over the sauce.

1 Cook the cauliflower in a saucepan of boiling salted water for 4–5 minutes. It should still be firm. Drain, place in a hot 1.4-litre/2½-pint gratin dish and keep warm.

2 Melt the butter in the rinsed-out saucepan over a medium heat and stir in the flour. Cook for 1 minute, stirring continuously.

3 Remove from the heat and stir in the milk gradually until you have a smooth consistency.

4 Return to a low heat and continue to stir while the sauce comes to the boil and thickens. Reduce the heat and simmer gently, stirring constantly, for about 3 minutes until the sauce is creamy and smooth.

5 Remove from the heat and stir in the Cheddar cheese and a good grating of the nutmeg. Taste and season well with salt and pepper.

6 Pour the hot sauce over the cauliflower, top with the Parmesan and place under a hot grill to brown. Serve immediately.

Grandmas in this day and age are jetting off or cruising all over the world. Travel is cheaper and easier than in the past, making it possible to visit far-off destinations with diverse cultures and foods. Countries like China, Mexico and the newly accessible Eastern European nations have all contributed to our varied cuisine. We have taken recipes from many different cultures and adapted them to our own way of eating. As our society becomes increasingly multicultural, ingredients for these types of recipes are becoming

GRANDMA'S TRAVELS

more readily available, not just from specialist shops but increasingly from main-stream supermarkets. Pasta has long been a favourite and spaghetti Bolognese is popular with adults and children alike. Pizza is an ideal finger food that can be made from scratch or using prepared pizza bases and topped with different ingredients so that everyone can choose their own. From further afield come chicken Kiev and beef goulash, together with chicken fajitas and chilli con carne, introducing newer flavours and spices into our diets. Chow mein and Chinese spare ribs, with their use of eastern flavours and foodstuffs, are also included in this chapter.

SPAGHETTI
BOLOGNESE

SERVES 4

1 tbsp olive oil
1 onion, finely chopped
2 garlic cloves, chopped
1 carrot, chopped
1 celery stick, chopped
50 g/1¾ oz pancetta or streaky bacon,
   diced
350 g/12 oz lean fresh beef mince

400 g/14 oz canned chopped tomatoes
2 tsp dried oregano
125 ml/4 fl oz red wine
2 tbsp tomato purée
salt and pepper
350 g/12 oz dried spaghetti
freshly grated Parmesan cheese,
   to serve (optional)

GRANDMA'S TIPS

This is the world's favourite spaghetti dish, loved by adults and children alike. A good sauce takes time to make, but it's worth the effort. Prepare double quantities and freeze in individual portions so that you always have some on hand for a quick meal. Some recipes add chicken livers or mushrooms – the choice is up to you. Serve this dish piping hot with lots of grated cheese.

1 Heat the oil in a large frying pan over a low heat. Add the onion and cook for 3 minutes.

2 Add the garlic, carrot, celery and pancetta to the pan and sauté for 3–4 minutes, or until just starting to brown.

3 Add the beef and cook over a high heat for another 3 minutes, or until the meat has browned.

4 Stir in the tomatoes, oregano and red wine and bring to the boil. Reduce the heat and simmer for about 45 minutes.

5 Stir in the tomato purée and season with salt and pepper.

6 Bring a large pan of lightly salted water to the boil over a medium heat. Add the pasta and cook for about 8–10 minutes, or until tender, but still firm to the bite. Drain thoroughly.

7 Transfer the pasta to 4 serving plates and pour over the sauce. Toss to mix well and serve with Parmesan cheese, if you wish.

SPAGHETTI WITH MEATBALLS

SERVES 6
1 potato, diced
salt and pepper
400 g/14 oz fresh beef mince
1 onion, finely chopped
1 egg
4 tbsp chopped fresh flat-leaf parsley
plain flour, for dusting

5 tbsp olive oil
400 ml/14 fl oz passata
2 tbsp tomato purée
450 g/1 lb dried spaghetti

to garnish
6 fresh basil leaves, shredded
Parmesan cheese shavings

GRANDMA'S TIPS

Meatballs are a traditional accompaniment to spaghetti. They can be made with minced beef as here or with minced lamb or pork. A variety of ingredients can be added to give the dish a distinct taste – garlic can be used, as can herbs like oregano or marjoram. If time is short, substitute fresh breadcrumbs for the potato.

1 Place the potato in a small pan, add cold water to cover and a pinch of salt and bring to the boil. Cook for 10–15 minutes, until tender, then drain. Either mash thoroughly with a potato masher or fork or pass through a potato ricer.

2 Combine the potato, beef, onion, egg and parsley in a bowl and season to taste with salt and pepper. Spread out the flour on a plate. With dampened hands, shape the meat mixture into walnut-size balls and roll in the flour. Shake off any excess.

3 Heat the oil in a heavy-based frying pan, add the meatballs and cook over a medium heat, stirring and turning frequently, for 8–10 minutes, until golden all over.

4 Add the passata and tomato purée and cook for a further 10 minutes, until the sauce is reduced and thickened.

5 Meanwhile, bring a large saucepan of lightly salted water to the boil. Add the pasta, bring back to the boil and cook for 8–10 minutes, until tender, but still firm to the bite.

6 Drain well and add to the meatball sauce, tossing well to coat. Transfer to a warm serving dish, garnish with the basil leaves and Parmesan and serve immediately.

FETTUCCINE ALFREDO

SERVES 4
2 tbsp butter
200 ml/7 fl oz double cream
salt and pepper
450 g/1 lb fresh fettuccine

85 g/3 oz freshly grated Parmesan
  cheese, plus extra to serve
pinch of freshly grated nutmeg
fresh flat-leaf parsley sprigs, to garnish

1 Put the butter and 150 ml/5 fl oz of the cream into a large pan and bring the mixture to the boil over a medium heat. Reduce the heat, then simmer gently for 1½ minutes, or until the cream has thickened slightly.

2 Meanwhile, bring a large pan of lightly salted water to the boil over medium heat. Add the pasta and cook for 2–3 minutes, or until tender, but still firm to the bite. Drain thoroughly and return to the pan, then pour over the cream sauce.

3 Toss the pasta in the sauce over a low heat, stirring with a wooden spoon, until coated thoroughly.

4 Add the remaining cream, Parmesan cheese and nutmeg to the pasta mixture and season to taste with salt and pepper. Toss the pasta in the mixture while heating through.

5 Transfer the pasta mixture to warmed serving bowls and garnish with fresh parsley sprigs. Serve immediately with extra grated Parmesan cheese.

LASAGNE AL FORNO

SERVES 4
2 tbsp olive oil
55 g/2 oz pancetta or rindless streaky
  bacon, chopped
1 onion, chopped
1 garlic clove, finely chopped
225 g/8 oz fresh beef mince
2 celery sticks, chopped
2 carrots, chopped
salt and pepper
pinch of sugar
½ tsp dried oregano
400 g/14 oz canned chopped tomatoes
225 g/8 oz dried no-precook lasagne
  sheets
115 g/4 oz freshly grated Parmesan
  cheese, plus extra for sprinkling

for the cheese sauce
300 ml/10 fl oz milk
1 bay leaf
6 black peppercorns
slice of onion
blade of mace
2 tbsp butter
3 tbsp plain flour
2 tsp Dijon mustard
70 g/2½ oz Cheddar cheese, grated
70 g/2½ oz Gruyère cheese, grated
salt and pepper

1 Preheat the oven to 190°C/375°F/Gas Mark 5. Heat the olive oil in a large, heavy-based saucepan. Add the pancetta and cook over a medium heat, stirring occasionally, for 3 minutes, or until the fat begins to run. Add the onion and garlic and cook, stirring occasionally, for 5 minutes, or until softened.

2 Add the beef and cook, breaking it up with a wooden spoon, until browned all over. Stir in the celery and carrots and cook for 5 minutes. Season to taste with salt and pepper. Add the sugar, oregano and tomatoes. Bring to the boil, reduce the heat and simmer for 30 minutes.

3 Meanwhile, make the cheese sauce. Pour the milk into a saucepan and add the bay leaf, peppercorns, onion and mace. Heat gently to just below the boiling point, then remove from the heat, cover and leave to infuse for 10 minutes. Strain the milk into a jug. Melt the butter in a separate saucepan. Sprinkle in the flour and cook over a low heat, stirring constantly, for 1 minute. Remove from the heat and gradually stir in the warm milk. Return to the heat and bring to the boil, stirring. Cook, stirring, until thickened and smooth. Stir in the mustard and both cheeses, then season to taste with salt and pepper.

4 In a large, rectangular ovenproof dish, make alternate layers of meat sauce, lasagne and Parmesan cheese. Pour the cheese sauce over the layers, covering them completely, and sprinkle with Parmesan cheese. Bake in the preheated oven for 30 minutes, or until golden brown and bubbling. Serve immediately.

PIZZA MARGHERITA

SERVES 4
for the pizza dough
15 g/½ oz easy-blend dried yeast
1 tsp sugar
250 ml/9 fl oz warm water
350 g/12 oz strong white flour, plus
    extra for dusting
1 tsp salt
1 tbsp olive oil, plus extra for oiling

for the topping
400 g/14 oz canned chopped tomatoes
2 garlic cloves, crushed
2 tsp dried basil
1 tbsp olive oil
salt and pepper
2 tbsp tomato purée
100 g/3½ oz mozzarella cheese, chopped
2 tbsp freshly grated Parmesan cheese

1 Place the yeast and sugar in a measuring jug and mix with 50 ml/2 fl oz of the water. Leave the yeast mixture in a warm place for 15 minutes or until frothy.

2 Mix the flour with the salt and make a well in the centre. Add the oil, the yeast mixture and the remaining water. Using a wooden spoon, mix to form a smooth dough.

3 Turn the dough out onto a floured surface and knead for 4–5 minutes or until smooth.

4 Return the dough to the bowl, cover with an oiled sheet of clingfilm and leave to rise for 30 minutes or until doubled in size.

5 Knead the dough for 2 minutes. Stretch the dough with your hands, then place it on an oiled baking tray or pizza stone, pushing out the edges until even. The dough should be no more than 6 mm/¼ inch thick because it will rise during cooking.

6 Preheat the oven to 200°C/400°F/Gas Mark 6. To make the topping, place the tomatoes, garlic, dried basil, olive oil and salt and pepper to taste in a large frying pan and leave to simmer for 20 minutes or until the sauce has thickened. Stir in the tomato purée and leave to cool slightly.

7 Spread the topping evenly over the pizza base. Top with the mozzarella and Parmesan cheeses and bake in the preheated oven for 20–25 minutes. Serve hot.

RATATOUILLE

SERVES 4
2 aubergines
4 courgettes
2 yellow peppers
2 red peppers
2 onions

2 garlic cloves
150 ml/5 fl oz olive oil
I bouquet garni
3 large tomatoes, peeled, deseeded and
    roughly chopped
salt and pepper

1 Roughly chop the aubergines and courgettes, and deseed and chop the peppers. Slice the onions and finely chop the garlic. Heat the oil in a large saucepan. Add the onions and cook over a low heat, stirring occasionally, for 5 minutes, or until softened. Add the garlic and cook, stirring frequently for a further 2 minutes.

2 Add the aubergines, courgettes and peppers. Increase the heat to medium and cook, stirring occasionally, until the peppers begin to colour. Add the bouquet garni, reduce the heat, cover and simmer gently for 40 minutes.

3 Stir in the chopped tomatoes and season to taste with salt and pepper. Re-cover the saucepan and simmer gently for a further 10 minutes. Remove and discard the bouquet garni. Serve warm or cold.

PAELLA

SERVES 4–6

1.2 litres/2 pints fish stock or water
12 large raw prawns, in their shells
½ tsp saffron threads
2 tbsp hot water
100 g/3½ oz skinless, boneless chicken
   breast, cut into ½-inch/1-cm pieces
100 g/3½ oz pork fillet, cut into ½-inch/
   1-cm pieces
salt and pepper
3 tbsp olive oil
100 g/3½ oz Spanish chorizo sausage,
   casing removed, cut into ½-inch/1-cm
   slices

1 large red onion, chopped
2 garlic cloves, crushed
½ tsp cayenne pepper
½ tsp paprika
1 red pepper, deseeded and sliced
1 green pepper, deseeded and sliced
12 cherry tomatoes, halved
350 g/12 oz medium-grain paella rice
1 tbsp chopped fresh parsley
2 tsp chopped fresh tarragon

GRANDMA'S TIPS

This traditional Spanish dish includes lots of ingredients, which is wonderful for a large party, but a simpler paella can be made using just chicken and prawns and would be great for everyday meals. Double the chicken and prawns in the recipe, and buy cooked prawns to save time. Follow the method, adding or omitting any vegetables as you wish.

1 Put the stock in a large pan and bring to a simmer. Add the prawns and cook for 2 minutes. Using a slotted spoon, transfer the prawns to a bowl and set aside. Let the stock simmer. Put the saffron threads and water in a small bowl or cup and let infuse for a few minutes.

2 Season the chicken and pork to taste with salt and pepper. Heat the oil in a paella pan or wide, shallow frying pan and cook the chicken, pork and chorizo over medium heat, stirring, for 5 minutes, or until golden. Add the onion and cook, stirring, for 2–3 minutes, or until softened. Add the garlic, cayenne pepper, paprika and saffron and its soaking liquid and cook, stirring constantly, for 1 minute. Add the pepper slices and tomato halves and cook, stirring, for a further 2 minutes.

3 Add the rice and herbs and cook, stirring constantly, for 1 minute, or until the rice is glossy and coated. Pour in all but 100 ml/3½ fl oz of the hot stock and bring to the boil. Reduce the heat and let simmer, uncovered, for 10 minutes. Do not stir during cooking, but shake the pan once or twice. Season to taste with salt and pepper, then shake the pan and cook for a further 10 minutes, or until the rice grains are plump and almost cooked. If the liquid is absorbed too quickly, pour in a little more hot stock, then shake the pan to spread the liquid through the paella. Do not stir it in. Add the prawns and shake the pan, but do not stir. Cook for a further 2 minutes.

4 When all the liquid has been absorbed and you detect a faint toasty aroma coming from the rice, remove from the heat immediately to prevent burning. Cover the pan with a clean tea towel or foil and let stand for 5 minutes. Divide the paella among warmed serving plates and serve immediately.

COQ AU VIN

SERVES 4
4 tbsp butter
2 tbsp olive oil
1.8 kg/4 lb chicken pieces
115 g/4 oz rindless smoked bacon,
   cut into strips
115 g/4 oz baby onions
115 g/4 oz chestnut mushrooms, halved

2 garlic cloves, finely chopped
2 tbsp brandy
225 ml/8 fl oz red wine
300 ml/10 fl oz chicken stock
1 bouquet garni
salt and pepper
2 tbsp plain flour
bay leaves, to garnish

GRANDMA'S TIPS

Coq au vin is usually made with red wine, but it also can be made with white wine like a Riesling. If you're using white wine, add 125 ml/4 fl oz of single cream before serving and garnish with freshly chopped parsley.

1 Melt half the butter with the olive oil in a large, flameproof casserole. Add the chicken and cook over a medium heat, stirring, for 8–10 minutes, or until golden brown all over. Add the bacon, onions, mushrooms and garlic.

2 Pour in the brandy and set it alight with a match or taper. When the flames have died down, add the wine, stock and bouquet garni and season to taste with salt and pepper. Bring to the boil, reduce the heat and simmer gently for 1 hour, or until the chicken pieces are cooked through and tender. Meanwhile, make a beurre manié by mashing the remaining butter with the flour in a small bowl.

3 Remove and discard the bouquet garni. Transfer the chicken to a large plate and keep warm. Stir the beurre manié into the casserole, a little at a time. Bring to the boil, return the chicken to the casserole and serve immediately, garnished with bay leaves.

BEEF BOURGUIGNON

SERVES 4–6

85 g/3 oz butter
2 tbsp sunflower oil
175 g/6 oz smoked lardons, blanched for
   30 seconds, drained and patted dry
900 g/2 lb braising beef, such as chuck
   or leg
2 large garlic cloves, crushed
1 carrot, diced
1 leek, halved and sliced
1 onion, finely chopped

2 tbsp plain flour
salt and pepper
350 ml/12 fl oz full-bodied red wine
about 500 ml/18 fl oz beef stock
1 tbsp tomato purée
1 bouquet garni
12 baby onions, peeled but kept whole
12 button mushrooms
chopped fresh flat-leaf parsley, to garnish
French bread, to serve

1 Preheat the oven to 150°C/300°F/Gas Mark 2. Heat 25 g/1 oz of the butter and
1 tablespoon of the oil in a large, flameproof casserole. Cook the lardons over a
medium-high heat, stirring, for 2 minutes, or until beginning to brown. Using a slotted
spoon, remove from the casserole and drain on kitchen paper.

2 Trim the beef and cut it into 5-cm/2-inch chunks. Add the beef to the casserole and
cook over a high heat, stirring frequently, for 5 minutes, or until browned on all sides
and sealed, adding more of the butter or oil to the casserole as necessary. Using a slotted
spoon, transfer the beef to a plate.

3 Pour off all but 2 tablespoons of the fat from the casserole. Add the garlic, carrot, leek
and onion and cook over a medium heat, stirring frequently, for 3 minutes, or until the
onion is beginning to soften. Sprinkle in the flour, season to taste with salt and pepper,
and cook, stirring constantly, for 2 minutes, then remove from the heat.

4 Gradually stir in the wine and stock and add the tomato purée and bouquet garni, then
return to the heat and bring to the boil, stirring and scraping any sediment from the base
of the casserole.

5 Return the beef and lardons to the casserole and add extra stock if necessary so that
the ingredients are covered by about 1 cm/1/2 inch of liquid. Slowly return to the boil,
then cover and cook in the preheated oven for 2 hours.

6 Meanwhile, heat 25 g/1 oz of the remaining butter and the remaining oil in a large
sauté pan or frying pan and cook the baby onions over a medium-high heat, stirring
frequently, until golden all over. Using a slotted spoon, transfer the onions to a plate.

7 Heat the remaining butter in the pan and cook the mushrooms, stirring frequently,
until golden brown. Remove from the pan and then stir them, with the onions, into the
casserole, re-cover and cook for a further 30 minutes, or until the beef is very tender.

8 Discard the bouquet garni, then adjust the seasoning to taste. Serve garnished with
parsley, accompanied by plenty of French bread for mopping up all the juices.

CHILLI CON CARNE

SERVES 4
1 tbsp sunflower or corn oil
1 small onion, roughly chopped
1 or 2 garlic cloves, roughly chopped
1 green pepper, deseeded and diced
225 g/8 oz fresh beef mince
1 tsp chilli powder
400 g/14 oz canned chopped tomatoes

½ tsp salt (optional)
400 g/14 oz canned kidney beans,
   drained and rinsed

to serve
grated cheese
freshly cooked rice
tortilla chips

GRANDMA'S TIPS

Always make sure you check the strength of the chilli powder you are using as it comes in different strengths. If you don't like your chilli too hot, use a mild powder and decrease the amount. Soured cream and guacamole are traditional accompaniments.

1 Heat the oil in a shallow frying pan over a low heat. Stir in the onion, garlic and green pepper and cook gently for 5 minutes.

2 Add the beef mince and stir well. Increase the heat to high and cook for 5 minutes, stirring occasionally. Spoon off any excess fat. Sprinkle over the chilli powder and mix well. Continue cooking for 2–3 minutes. Stir in the tomatoes, reduce the heat, cover and cook gently for at least 30 minutes. You may need to add a little water or beef stock if it starts to dry out.

3 Halfway through the cooking time check the seasoning and stir in the salt if needed. Add more chilli powder to taste, but be careful not to use too much.

4 Add the drained kidney beans to the chilli mixture 5–10 minutes before the end of the cooking time so that they heat through with the meat and spices.

5 Serve immediately topped with a little grated cheese and accompanied by freshly cooked rice and tortilla chips.

CHICKEN FAJITAS

SERVES 4

3 tbsp olive oil, plus extra for drizzling
3 tbsp maple syrup or clear honey
1 tbsp red wine vinegar
2 garlic cloves, crushed
2 tsp dried oregano

1–2 tsp dried red chilli flakes
salt and pepper
4 chicken breasts, skinless, boneless
2 red peppers, deseeded and cut into
    2.5-cm/1-inch strips
8 flour tortillas, warmed

GRANDMA'S TIPS

Tortillas can be heated by wrapping in foil and placing in a warm oven for 3–4 minutes. Your family will enjoy wrapping their own fajitas – provide bowls of shredded lettuce, tomato salsa and soured cream to choose from.

1 Place the oil, maple syrup, vinegar, garlic, oregano, chilli flakes and salt and pepper to taste in a large, shallow dish or bowl and mix together.

2 Slice the chicken across the grain into slices 2.5 cm/1 inch thick. Toss in the marinade until well coated. Cover and leave to chill in the refrigerator for 2–3 hours, turning occasionally.

3 Heat a griddle pan until hot. Lift the chicken slices from the marinade with a slotted spoon, lay on the griddle pan and cook over medium-high heat for 3–4 minutes on each side, or until cooked through. Remove the chicken to a warmed serving plate and keep warm.

4 Add the peppers, skin side down, to the griddle pan and cook for 2 minutes on each side. Transfer to the serving plate.

5 Serve immediately with the warmed tortillas to be used as wraps.

CHICKEN TIKKA MASALA

SERVES 6

½ onion, roughly chopped
55 g/2 oz tomato purée
1 tsp cumin seeds
2.5-cm/1-inch piece fresh root ginger, chopped
3 tbsp lemon juice
2 garlic cloves, crushed
2 tsp chilli powder
750 g/1 lb 10 oz boneless chicken
salt and pepper
fresh mint sprigs, to garnish

for the masala sauce

2 tbsp ghee
1 onion, sliced
1 tbsp black onion seeds
3 garlic cloves, crushed
2 fresh green chillies, chopped
200 g/7 oz canned chopped tomatoes
125 ml/4 fl oz low-fat natural yogurt
125 ml/4 fl oz coconut milk
1 tbsp chopped fresh coriander
1 tbsp chopped fresh mint
2 tbsp lemon or lime juice
½ tsp garam masala

1 Combine the onion, tomato purée, cumin seeds, ginger, lemon juice, garlic and chilli powder in a food processor or blender and transfer to a bowl. Season to taste with salt and pepper. Cut chicken into 4-cm/1½-inch cubes. Stir into the bowl and leave for 2 hours.

2 Make the masala sauce. Heat the ghee in a saucepan, add the onion and stir over a medium heat for 5 minutes. Add the black onion seeds, garlic and chillies. Add the tomatoes, yogurt and coconut milk, bring to the boil, then simmer for 20 minutes.

3 Divide the chicken evenly between 8 oiled skewers and cook under a very hot preheated grill for 15 minutes, turning frequently. Remove the chicken and add to the sauce. Stir in the herbs, lemon juice and garam masala. Serve garnished with mint sprigs.

VEGETABLE KORMA

SERVES 4
4 tbsp ghee or vegetable oil
2 onions, chopped
2 garlic cloves, chopped
1 fresh red chilli, chopped
1 tbsp grated fresh root ginger
2 tomatoes, peeled and chopped
1 orange pepper, deseeded and cut into
   small pieces
1 large potato, cut into chunks
200 g/7 oz cauliflower florets

½ tsp salt
1 tsp ground turmeric
1 tsp ground cumin
1 tsp ground coriander
1 tsp garam masala
200 ml/7 fl oz vegetable stock or water
150 ml/5 fl oz natural yogurt
150 ml/5 fl oz single cream
25 g/1 oz fresh coriander, chopped
freshly cooked rice, to serve

GRANDMA'S TIPS
*Try using other vegetables, such
as green beans, okra, carrots
and aubergines, to give a variety
of flavours and textures. If you
don't have all the spices just add
2 teaspoons of curry paste – or
more if you are feeling brave!*

1 Heat the ghee in a large saucepan over a medium heat, add the onions and garlic and cook, stirring, for 3 minutes. Add the chilli and ginger and cook for a further 4 minutes. Add the tomatoes, pepper, potato, cauliflower, salt and spices and cook, stirring, for a further 3 minutes. Stir in the stock and bring to the boil. Reduce the heat and simmer for 25 minutes.

2 Stir in the yogurt and cream and cook, stirring, for a further 5 minutes. Add the fresh coriander and heat through.

3 Serve the curry with freshly cooked rice.

CHICKEN KIEV

SERVES 4
4 tbsp butter, softened
1 garlic clove, finely chopped
1 tbsp finely chopped fresh parsley
  plus extra sprigs to garnish
1 tbsp finely chopped fresh oregano
salt and pepper
4 skinless, boneless chicken breasts
85 g/3 oz fresh white or wholemeal
  breadcrumbs

3 tbsp freshly grated Parmesan cheese
1 egg, beaten
250 ml/9 fl oz vegetable oil, for
  deep-frying

to serve
freshly cooked new potatoes
selection of cooked vegetables

GRANDMA'S TIPS
*Chill the herb butter well before
using so that it won't melt too
quickly during cooking. Sautéed
sliced mushrooms or sun-dried
tomatoes can be added to the
butter for an interesting twist.*

1 Place the butter and garlic in a bowl and mix together well. Stir in the chopped herbs and season well with salt and pepper. Pound the chicken breasts to flatten them to an even thickness, then place a tablespoon of herb butter in the centre of each one. Fold in the sides to enclose the butter, then secure with cocktail sticks.

2 Combine the breadcrumbs and grated Parmesan on a plate. Dip the chicken parcels into the beaten egg, then coat in the breadcrumb mixture. Transfer to a plate, cover and chill for 30 minutes. Remove from the refrigerator and coat in the egg and then the breadcrumb mixture for a second time.

3 Pour the oil into a deep-fat fryer to a depth that will cover the chicken parcels. Heat until it reaches 180–190°C/350–375°F, or until a cube of bread browns in 30 seconds. Transfer the chicken to the hot oil and deep-fry for 5 minutes, or until cooked through. Lift out the chicken and drain on kitchen paper.

4 Divide the chicken among 4 serving plates, garnish with parsley sprigs and serve with new potatoes and a selection of vegetables.

BEEF GOULASH

SERVES 4

2 tbsp vegetable oil
1 large onion, chopped
1 garlic clove, crushed
750 g/1 lb 10 oz lean braising beef
2 tbsp paprika
400 g/14 oz canned chopped tomatoes
2 tbsp tomato purée
1 large red pepper, deseeded and
   chopped

175 g/6 oz button mushrooms, sliced
600 ml/1 pint beef stock
1 tbsp cornflour
1 tbsp water
salt and pepper
chopped fresh parsley, to garnish
freshly cooked long-grain and wild rice,
   to serve

1 Heat the vegetable oil in a large, heavy-based frying pan. Add the onion and garlic and cook over a low heat for 3–4 minutes.

2 Using a sharp knife, cut the beef into chunks, add to the frying pan and cook over a high heat for 3 minutes, or until browned. Add the paprika and stir well, then add the tomatoes, tomato purée, red pepper and mushrooms. Cook for a further 2 minutes, stirring frequently. Pour in the stock. Bring to the boil, reduce the heat, cover and simmer for 1^1/$_2$–2 hours, or until the meat is tender.

3 Blend the cornflour and water together in a small bowl, then add to the frying pan, stirring, until thickened and smooth. Cook for 1 minute. Season to taste with salt and pepper.

4 Transfer the beef goulash to a warmed serving dish, garnish with chopped fresh parsley and serve with a mix of long-grain and wild rice.

MUSHROOM
STROGANOFF

SERVES 4

550 g/1 lb 4 oz mixed fresh mushrooms, such as chanterelles, chestnut, ceps and oyster
1 red onion, diced
2 garlic cloves, crushed
425 ml/15 fl oz vegetable stock
1 tbsp tomato purée

2 tbsp lemon juice
15 g/½ oz cornflour
2 tbsp cold water
115 g/4 oz low-fat natural yogurt
3 tbsp chopped fresh parsley
freshly ground black pepper
freshly cooked brown or white rice, to serve

1 Put the mushrooms, onion, garlic, stock, tomato purée and lemon juice into a saucepan and bring to the boil. Reduce the heat, cover and simmer for 15 minutes, or until the onion is tender.

2 Blend the cornflour with the water in a small bowl and stir into the mushroom mixture. Return to the boil, stirring constantly, and cook until the sauce thickens. Reduce the heat and simmer for a further 2–3 minutes, stirring occasionally.

3 Just before serving, remove the saucepan from the heat and stir in the yogurt, making sure that the stroganoff is not boiling or it may separate and curdle. Stir in 2 tablespoons of the parsley and season to taste with pepper. Transfer the stroganoff to a warmed serving dish, sprinkle over the remaining parsley and serve immediately with freshly cooked brown or white rice.

SWEET & SOUR PRAWNS

SERVES 4
450 g/1 lb cooked tiger prawns
1 tbsp groundnut or sunflower oil
4 spring onions, finely chopped
2 tsp finely chopped fresh root ginger
2 tbsp dark soy sauce
2 tbsp muscovado sugar
3 tbsp rice vinegar

1 tbsp Chinese rice wine
125 ml/4 fl oz fish or chicken stock
1 tsp cornflour
1–2 tbsp water
dash of sesame oil
shredded Chinese leaves, to serve
shredded spring onion, to garnish

GRANDMA'S TIPS

For a change, try making this dish with pork fillet instead of prawns. Finely slice the pork into medallions and fry in the wok or large frying pan, turning occasionally until cooked through. Then add the other ingredients as the recipe directs.

1 Peel and devein the prawns, pat dry with kitchen paper and reserve.

2 Heat the oil in a preheated wok or large frying pan. Add the spring onions and ginger and stir-fry over a high heat for 1 minute. Add the soy sauce, sugar, vinegar, rice wine and stock and bring to the boil.

3 Place the cornflour and water in a small bowl and mix to make a paste. Stir 1 tablespoon of the paste into the sauce and add the prawns. Cook, stirring, until slightly thickened and smooth. Sprinkle with sesame oil.

4 Make a bed of Chinese leaves in 4 serving bowls and top with prawns and sauce. Garnish with the shredded spring onion and serve immediately.

PORK CHOW MEIN

SERVES 4
250 g/9 oz egg noodles
4–5 tbsp vegetable oil
250 g/9 oz pork fillet, cooked
125g/4½ oz French beans
2 tbsp light soy sauce

1 tsp salt
½ tsp sugar
1 tbsp Chinese rice wine or dry sherry
2 spring onions, finely shredded
a few drops sesame oil
chilli sauce, to serve (optional)

1 Cook the noodles in boiling water according to the instructions on the packet, then drain and rinse under cold water. Drain again then toss with 1 tablespoon of the oil.

2 Slice the pork into thin shreds and trim the beans.

3 Heat 3 tablespoons of the oil in a preheated wok until hot. Add the noodles and stir-fry for 2–3 minutes with 1 tablespoon of the soy sauce, then remove to a serving dish. Keep warm.

4 Heat the remaining oil and stir-fry the beans and meat for 2 minutes. Add the salt, sugar, rice wine, the remaining soy sauce and about half of the spring onions to the wok.

5 Stir the mixture in the wok, adding a little stock if necessary, then pour on top of the noodles, and sprinkle with sesame oil and the remaining spring onions.

6 Serve the chow mein hot or cold with chilli sauce, if using.

CHINESE SPARE RIBS

SERVES 4

1 kg/2 lb 4 oz pork spare ribs, separated
4 tbsp dark soy sauce
3 tbsp muscovado sugar
1 tbsp groundnut or sunflower oil

2 garlic cloves, finely chopped
2 tsp Chinese five-spice powder
1-cm/½-inch piece fresh root ginger, grated
shredded spring onions, to serve

GRANDMA'S TIPS

An easy way to marinate meat is to put it into a large plastic bag. Pour in the marinade, seal the bag and shake well. Refrigerate overnight. During the last 15 minutes of cooking do not baste with marinades that have been in contact with raw meat. A safer way would be to reserve a portion of the marinade for basting before adding the spare ribs.

1 Place the spare ribs in a large, shallow, non-metallic dish. Mix the soy sauce, sugar, oil, garlic, Chinese five-spice powder and ginger together in a bowl. Pour the mixture over the ribs and turn until the ribs are thoroughly coated in the marinade.

2 Cover the dish with clingfilm and leave to marinate in the refrigerator for at least 6 hours.

3 Preheat the barbecue. Drain the ribs, reserving the marinade. Cook over medium-hot coals, turning and brushing frequently with the reserved marinade, for 30–40 minutes. Transfer to a large serving dish, garnish with the shredded spring onions and serve immediately.

Christmas and other holidays were always when Grandma came into her own. She would love having her family around her and always pulled out all the stops to give them the best of everything. Starters of special soups and pâté are included in this chapter and there are, of course, recipes for roast turkey and the all-important stuffing. Ham, goose and beef wellington recipes are also provided as alternatives to the turkey but they are just as good for winter dinners – and the salmon dish is ideal for a summer's day too.

GRANDMA'S FESTIVE FARE

Vegetarians are not forgotten as there is a mixed nut roast to be served with a cranberry and red wine sauce, and some delicious individual vegetable dishes too. Those with a sweet tooth will not be disappointed either, as there are two very special desserts to choose from – either the customary Christmas pudding or a festive sherry trifle. These recipes can be used at other times of the year to celebrate any festival in the calendar or special family event, like a birth, christening or birthday.

WILD MUSHROOM & SHERRY SOUP

SERVES 4
2 tbsp olive oil
1 onion, chopped
1 garlic clove, chopped
125 g/4½ oz sweet potato, peeled and chopped
1 leek, trimmed and sliced
200 g/7 oz chestnut mushrooms
150 g/5½ oz mixed wild mushrooms

600 ml/1 pint vegetable stock
350 ml/12 fl oz single cream
4 tbsp sherry
salt and pepper

to garnish/serve
Parmesan cheese shavings
sautéed sliced wild mushrooms
fresh crusty bread

GRANDMA'S TIPS

When you can only find cultivated mushrooms, increase the flavour of the dish by adding some dried porcini mushrooms. Rehydrate the porcini in a little hot water to cover for 15–20 minutes and then add both the porcini and their soaking liquid to the soup.

1 Heat the oil in a saucepan over a medium heat. Add the onion and garlic and cook, stirring, for 3 minutes until softened slightly. Add the sweet potato and cook for another 3 minutes. Stir in the leek and cook for another 2 minutes.

2 Stir in the mushrooms, stock and cream. Bring to the boil, then reduce the heat and simmer gently, stirring occasionally, for about 25 minutes. Remove from the heat, stir in the sherry, and leave to cool a little.

3 Transfer half of the soup into a food processor and blend until smooth. Return the mixture to the pan with the rest of the soup, season with salt and pepper and reheat gently, stirring. Pour into 4 warmed soup bowls, garnish with Parmesan shavings and sautéed wild mushrooms, and serve with fresh crusty bread.

SPICED PUMPKIN SOUP

SERVES 4
2 tbsp olive oil
I onion, chopped
I garlic clove, chopped
I tbsp chopped fresh root ginger
I small red chilli, deseeded and finely
   chopped

2 tbsp chopped fresh coriander
I bay leaf
I kg/2 lb 4 oz pumpkin, peeled, deseeded
   and diced
600 ml/I pint vegetable stock
salt and pepper
single cream, to garnish

GRANDMA'S TIPS

Pumpkins are often tough-skinned and difficult to handle. The easiest way to prepare a pumpkin or squash is to cut it into quarters using a sharp knife, then remove the seeds and cut into smaller pieces. These pieces will then be easier to peel, either using a sharp knife or a potato peeler. Occasionally you might find some prepared pumpkin in the supermarket, which makes things easier still.

1 Heat the oil in a saucepan over a medium heat. Add the onion and garlic and cook, stirring, for about 4 minutes, until slightly softened. Add the ginger, chilli, coriander, bay leaf and pumpkin and cook for another 3 minutes.

2 Pour in the stock and bring to the boil. Using a slotted spoon, skim any scum from the surface. Reduce the heat and simmer gently, stirring occasionally, for about 25 minutes, or until the pumpkin is tender. Remove from the heat, take out the bay leaf and leave to cool a little.

3 Transfer the soup into a food processor and blend until smooth (you may have to do this in batches). Return the mixture to the pan and season with salt and pepper. Reheat gently, stirring. Remove from the heat, pour into 4 warmed soup bowls, garnish each one with a swirl of cream and serve.

CHICKEN LIVER PÂTÉ

SERVES 4–6
200 g/7 oz butter
225 g/8 oz trimmed chicken livers,
  thawed if frozen
2 tbsp Marsala or brandy
1 ½ tsp chopped fresh sage

1 garlic clove, coarsely chopped
150 ml/5 fl oz double cream
salt and pepper
fresh bay leaves or sage leaves,
  to garnish
crackers, to serve

1 Melt 40 g/1½ oz of the butter in a large, heavy-based frying pan. Add the chicken livers and cook over a medium heat for about 4 minutes on each side. They should be browned on the outside but still pink in the middle. Transfer to a food processor and process until finely chopped.

2 Stir the Marsala or brandy into the pan, scraping up any sediment with a wooden spoon, then add to the food processor with the chopped sage, garlic and 100 g/3½ oz of the remaining butter. Process until smooth. Add the cream, season with salt and pepper and process until thoroughly combined and smooth. Spoon the pâté into a dish or individual ramekins, smooth the surface and leave to cool completely.

3 Melt the remaining butter, then spoon it over the surface of the pâté. Decorate with herb leaves, cool, then chill in the refrigerator. Serve with crackers.

STILTON & WALNUT TARTLETS

MAKES 12
for the pastry
225 g/8 oz plain flour, plus extra
    for dusting
pinch of celery salt
100 g/3½ oz cold butter, cut into pieces,
    plus extra for greasing
25 g/1 oz walnut halves, chopped in a
    food processor
cold water

for the filling
25g/1oz butter
2 celery sticks, trimmed and finely
    chopped
1 small leek, trimmed and finely chopped
200 ml/7 fl oz double cream, plus 2 tbsp
    extra
200 g/7 oz Stilton
salt and pepper
3 egg yolks

GRANDMA'S TIPS
To make these delicious tartlets more quickly you can use ready-made shortcrust pastry. The tartlets obviously won't have the walnut flavour or texture, but the filling will be just as tasty.

1 Lightly butter a 7.5-cm/3-inch, 12-hole muffin tray. Sift the flour and celery salt into a food processor, add the butter and process until the mixture resembles fine breadcrumbs. Tip the mixture into a large bowl and add the walnuts and a little cold water, just enough to bring the dough together. Turn out on to a floured surface and cut the dough in half. Roll out the first piece and cut out six 9-cm/3½-inch circles. Take each circle and roll out to 12 cm/4½ inches diameter and fit into the muffin holes, pressing to fill the holes. Do the same with the remaining dough. Put a piece of baking paper in each hole, fill with baking beans then put the tray in the refrigerator to chill for 30 minutes. Meanwhile, preheat the oven to 200°C/400°F/Gas Mark 6.

2 Remove the muffin tray from the refrigerator and bake the tartlets blind for 10 minutes in the preheated oven then carefully remove the paper and beans.

3 Melt the butter in a frying pan and add the celery and leek and cook for 15 minutes, until soft. Add 2 tablespoons of the double cream and crumble in the Stilton, mix well and season with salt and pepper. Bring the remaining cream to a simmer in another pan, then pour on to the egg yolks, stirring all the time. Mix in the Stilton mixture and spoon into the pastry cases. Bake for 10 minutes then turn the tray around in the oven and bake for a further 5 minutes. Cool in the tin for 5 minutes before serving.

SMOKED SALMON, DILL &
HORSERADISH TARTLETS

MAKES 6
for the pastry
125 g/4½ oz plain flour, plus extra for
    dusting
pinch of salt
75 g/2½ oz cold butter, cut into pieces,
    plus extra for greasing
cold water

for the filling
125 ml/4 fl oz crème fraîche
1 tsp creamed horseradish
½ tsp lemon juice
1 tsp Spanish capers, chopped
salt and pepper
3 egg yolks
200 g/7 oz smoked salmon trimmings
bunch fresh dill, chopped, plus extra
    sprigs to garnish

GRANDMA'S TIPS

If you're short of time, you can use ready-made shortcrust pastry to make the tartlets or you can use ready-made tartlet cases instead. The filling can also be used to make one larger (20-cm/8-inch) tart if you prefer – just increase the baking time to 20–25 minutes.

1 Butter six 9-cm/3½-inch loose-bottomed fluted tart tins. Sift the flour and salt into a food processor, add the butter and process until the mixture resembles fine breadcrumbs. Tip the mixture into a large bowl and add a little cold water, just enough to bring the dough together. Turn out on to a floured surface and divide into 6 equal-sized pieces. Roll each piece to fit the tart tins. Carefully fit each piece of pastry in its case and press well to fit the tin. Roll the rolling pin over the tin to neaten the edges and trim the excess pastry. Cut 6 pieces of baking paper and fit a piece into each tartlet, fill with baking beans and chill in the refrigerator for 30 minutes. Meanwhile, preheat the oven to 200°C/400°F/Gas Mark 6.

2 Bake the tart cases blind for 10 minutes in the preheated oven then remove the beans and baking paper.

3 Meanwhile, put the crème fraîche, horseradish, lemon juice, capers and salt and pepper into a bowl and mix well. Add the egg yolks, the smoked salmon and the dill and carefully mix again. Divide this mixture among the tartlet cases and return to the oven for 10 minutes. Cool in the tins for 5 minutes before serving garnished with dill sprigs.

ROAST TURKEY
WITH STUFFING

SERVES 8
1 x 5-kg/11-lb turkey
55 g/2 oz butter
5 tbsp red wine
400 ml/14 fl oz chicken stock
1 tbsp cornflour
1 tsp French mustard
1 tsp sherry vinegar

for the stuffing
225 g/8 oz pork sausagemeat
225 g/8 oz unsweetened chestnut purée
85 g/3 oz walnuts
115 g/4 oz dried apricots, chopped
2 tbsp chopped fresh parsley
2 tbsp chopped fresh chives
2 tsp chopped fresh sage
4–5 tbsp double cream
salt and pepper

1 To make the stuffing, combine the sausagemeat and chestnut purée in a bowl, then stir in the walnuts, apricots, parsley, chives and sage. Stir in enough cream to make a firm, but not dry, mixture. Season with salt and pepper.

2 Preheat the oven to 220°C/425°F/Gas Mark 7. If you are planning to stuff the turkey, fill only the neck cavity and close the flap of skin with a skewer. Alternatively, the stuffing may be cooked separately, either rolled into small balls or spooned into an ovenproof dish, for the last 30–40 minutes of the cooking time.

3 Place the bird in a large roasting tin and rub all over with 40 g/1½ oz of the butter. Roast for 1 hour, then lower the oven temperature to 180°C/350°F/Gas Mark 4 and roast for an additional 2½ hours. You may need to pour off the fat from the roasting tin occasionally.

4 Check that the turkey is cooked by inserting a skewer or the point of a sharp knife into the thigh; if the juices run clear, it is ready. Transfer the bird to a carving board, cover loosely with foil, and let rest.

5 To make the gravy, skim off the fat from the roasting tin then place the pan over a medium heat. Add the red wine and stir with a wooden spoon, scraping up the sediment from the bottom of the pan. Stir in the chicken stock. Mix the cornflour, mustard, vinegar, and 2 teaspoons of water together in a small bowl, then stir into the wine and stock. Bring to the boil, stirring constantly until thickened and smooth. Stir in the remaining butter.

6 Carve the turkey and serve with the stuffing and gravy.

YULETIDE GOOSE
WITH HONEY & PEARS

SERVES 4
1 x oven-ready goose, weighing
   3.5–4.5 kg/7 lb 12 oz–10 lb
1 tsp salt
4 pears

1 tbsp lemon juice
55 g/2 oz butter
2 tbsp clear honey
seasonal vegetables, to serve

1 Preheat the oven to 220°C/425°F/Gas Mark 7.

2 Rinse the goose and pat dry. Use a fork to prick the skin all over, then rub with the salt. Place the bird upside down on a rack in a roasting tin. Roast in the oven for 30 minutes. Drain off the fat. Turn the bird over and roast for 15 minutes. Drain off the fat. Reduce the temperature to 180°C/350°F/Gas Mark 4 and roast for 15 minutes per 450 g/1 lb. Cover with foil 15 minutes before the end of the cooking time. Check that the bird is cooked by inserting a knife between the legs and body. If the juices run clear, it is cooked. Remove from the oven.

3 Peel and halve the pears and brush with lemon juice. Melt the butter and honey in a saucepan over a low heat, then add the pears. Cook, stirring, for 5–10 minutes until tender. Remove from the heat, arrange the pears around the goose and pour the sweet juices over the bird. Serve with seasonal vegetables.

GLAZED GAMMON

SERVES 8
1 x 4-kg/9-lb gammon
1 apple, cored and chopped
1 onion, chopped
300 ml/10 fl oz cider

6 black peppercorns
1 bouquet garni
1 bay leaf
about 50 cloves
4 tbsp demerara sugar

1 Put the gammon in a large saucepan and add enough cold water to cover. Bring to the boil and skim off the scum that rises to the surface. Reduce the heat and simmer for 30 minutes. Drain the gammon and return to the saucepan. Add the apple, onion, cider, peppercorns, bouquet garni, bay leaf and a few of the cloves. Pour in enough fresh water to cover and bring back to the boil. Cover and simmer for 3 hours 20 minutes.

2 Preheat the oven to 200°C/400°F/Gas Mark 6. Take the saucepan off the heat and set aside to cool slightly. Remove the gammon from the cooking liquid and, while it is still warm, loosen the rind with a sharp knife, then peel it off and discard. Score the fat into diamond shapes and stud with the remaining cloves. Place the gammon on a rack in a roasting tin and sprinkle with the sugar. Roast, basting occasionally with the cooking liquid, for 20 minutes. Serve hot or cold.

FESTIVE BEEF
WELLINGTON

SERVES 4
750 g/1 lb 10 oz thick beef fillet
2 tbsp butter
salt and pepper
2 tbsp vegetable oil
1 garlic clove, chopped

1 onion, chopped
175 g/6 oz chestnut mushrooms
1 tbsp chopped fresh sage
350 g/12 oz frozen puff pastry, defrosted
1 egg, beaten

1 Preheat the oven to 220°C/425°F/Gas Mark 7. Put the beef in a roasting tin, spread with butter and season with salt and pepper. Roast for 30 minutes, then remove from the oven. Meanwhile, heat the oil in a pan over a medium heat. Add the garlic and onion and cook, stirring, for 3 minutes. Stir in the mushrooms, sage and salt and pepper to taste and cook for 5 minutes. Remove from the heat.

2 Roll out the pastry into a rectangle large enough to enclose the beef, then place the beef in the middle and spread the mushroom mixture over it. Bring the long sides of the pastry together over the beef and seal with beaten egg. Tuck the short ends over (trim away excess pastry) and seal. Place on a baking sheet, seam-side down. Make 2 slits in the top. Decorate with dough shapes and brush with beaten egg. Bake for 40 minutes. If the pastry browns too quickly, cover with foil. Remove from the oven, cut into thick slices and serve hot.

RACK OF LAMB

SERVES 2
1 trimmed rack of lamb, weighing
   250–300 g/9–10½ oz
1 garlic clove, crushed
150 ml/5 fl oz red wine
1 fresh rosemary sprig, crushed to
   release the flavour
salt and pepper
1 tbsp olive oil
150 ml/5 fl oz lamb stock
2 tbsp redcurrant jelly

for the mint sauce
bunch fresh mint leaves
2 tsp caster sugar
2 tbsp boiling water
2 tbsp white wine vinegar

GRANDMA'S TIPS

*This is an ideal roast to make
for just two people. For more,
double or treble the quantity.
It makes a very good dinner
party dish and is easy to carve.
Serve with a mixture of spring
vegetables and garnish with
rosemary.*

1 Place the rack of lamb in a non-metallic bowl and rub all over with the garlic. Pour over the wine and place the rosemary sprig on top. Cover and leave to marinate in the refrigerator for 3 hours or overnight if possible.

2 Preheat the oven to 220°C/425°F/Gas Mark 7. Remove the lamb from the marinade, reserving the marinade. Pat the meat dry with kitchen paper and season well with salt and pepper. Place it in a small roasting tin, drizzle with the oil and roast for 15–20 minutes, depending on whether you like your meat pink or medium. Remove the lamb from the oven and leave to rest, covered with foil, in a warm place for 5 minutes.

3 Meanwhile, pour the reserved marinade into a small saucepan, bring to the boil over a medium heat and boil rapidly for 5 minutes. Add the stock and redcurrant jelly and simmer, stirring, until the mixture is syrupy.

4 To make the mint sauce, chop the fresh mint leaves and mix together with the sugar in a small bowl. Add the boiling water and stir to dissolve the sugar. Add the white wine vinegar and leave to stand for 30 minutes before serving with the lamb.

5 Carve the lamb into cutlets and serve on warmed plates with the sauce spooned over the top. Serve the mint sauce separately.

HERBED SALMON WITH HOLLANDAISE SAUCE

SERVES 4
4 salmon fillets, about 175 g/6 oz each,
   skin removed
salt and pepper
2 tbsp olive oil
1 tbsp chopped fresh dill
1 tbsp chopped fresh chives, plus extra
   for garnish

for the hollandaise sauce
3 egg yolks
1 tbsp water
salt and pepper
225 g/8 oz butter, cut into small cubes
juice of 1 lemon

to serve
freshly boiled new potatoes
freshly cooked broccoli
sesame seeds, for sprinkling (optional)

GRANDMA'S TIPS

Hollandaise is a difficult sauce to make, as tends to separate. To simplify, boil the water with the lemon juice in a small pan. Place the egg yolks with the salt in a liquidiser and blend. With the motor running, pour the lemon juice mixture onto the egg yolks and blend. Melt the butter and add it to the blender in a steady stream until the mixture is thick. Hollandaise sauce should be served immediately after it has been made.

1 Preheat the grill to medium. Rinse the fish fillets under cold running water and pat dry with kitchen paper. Season with salt and pepper. Combine the olive oil with the dill and chives, then brush the mixture over the fish. Transfer to the grill and cook for about 6–8 minutes, turning once and brushing with more oil and herb mixture, until cooked to your taste.

2 Meanwhile, to make the hollandaise sauce, put the egg yolks in a heatproof bowl over a pan of boiling water (or use a double boiler). Add the water and season with salt and pepper. Lower the heat and simmer, whisking constantly, until the mixture begins to thicken. Whisk in the butter, cube by cube, until the mixture is thick and shiny. Whisk in the lemon juice, then remove from the heat.

3 Remove the fish from the grill and transfer to individual serving plates. Pour over the sauce and garnish with chopped fresh chives. Serve with freshly boiled new potatoes and broccoli, and sprinkle with sesame seeds, if using.

MIXED NUT ROAST WITH CRANBERRY & RED WINE SAUCE

SERVES 4

2 tbsp butter, plus extra for greasing
2 garlic cloves, chopped
1 large onion, chopped
50 g/1¾ oz pine kernels, toasted
75 g/2¾ oz hazelnuts, toasted
50 g/1¾ oz walnuts, ground
50 g/1¾ oz cashew nuts, ground
100 g/3½ oz wholemeal breadcrumbs
1 egg, lightly beaten

2 tbsp chopped fresh thyme
250 ml/9 fl oz vegetable stock
salt and pepper
sprigs of fresh thyme, to garnish

for the cranberry & red wine sauce
175 g/6 oz fresh cranberries
100 g/3½ oz caster sugar
300 ml/10 fl oz red wine
1 cinnamon stick

1 Preheat the oven to 180°C/350°F/Gas Mark 4. Grease a loaf tin and line it with greaseproof paper. Melt the butter in a saucepan over a medium heat. Add the garlic and onion and cook, stirring, for about 3 minutes. Remove the pan from the heat. Grind the pine kernels and hazelnuts. Stir all the nuts into the pan and add the breadcrumbs, egg, thyme, stock and seasoning.

2 Spoon the mixture into the loaf tin and level the surface. Cook in the centre of the preheated oven for 30 minutes or until cooked through and golden. The loaf is cooked when a skewer inserted into the centre comes out clean. Halfway through the cooking time, make the cranberry and red wine sauce. Put all the ingredients in a saucepan and bring to the boil. Reduce the heat and simmer, stirring occasionally, for 15 minutes.

3 Remove the nut roast from the oven and turn out. Garnish with sprigs of thyme and serve with the cranberry and red wine sauce.

PERFECT ROAST
POTATOES

SERVES 6
1.3 kg/3 lb large floury potatoes, such as
King Edwards, Maris Piper or Desirée,
peeled and cut into even-sized chunks

salt
3 tbsp goose fat, duck fat or olive oil

GRANDMA'S TIPS

*The potatoes can be seasoned
while they're roasting, which
allows the flavours to be
absorbed. Parsnips can also be
roasted in the same way but
they'll only need 2–3 minutes'
precooking and they don't need
to be shaken in the pan.*

1 Preheat the oven to 220°C/425°F/Gas Mark 7.

2 Cook the potatoes in a large saucepan of lightly salted boiling water over a medium heat, covered, for 5–7 minutes. They will still be firm. Remove from the heat. Meanwhile, add the fat to a roasting tin and place in the hot oven.

3 Drain the potatoes well and return them to the saucepan. Cover with the lid and firmly shake the pan so that the surface of the potatoes is slightly roughened to help give a much crisper texture.

4 Remove the roasting tin from the oven and carefully tip the potatoes into the hot fat. Baste them to ensure that they are all coated with it.

5 Roast the potatoes at the top of the oven for 45–50 minutes until they are browned all over and thoroughly crisp. Turn the potatoes and baste again only once during the process or the crunchy edges will be destroyed.

6 Using a slotted spoon, carefully transfer the potatoes from the roasting tin into a warmed serving dish. Sprinkle with a little salt and serve immediately. Any leftovers (although this is most unlikely) are delicious cold.

GLAZED TURNIPS

SERVES 4–6
900 g/2 lb young turnips, peeled and
    quartered
salt and pepper
55 g/2 oz butter

1 tbsp brown sugar
150 ml/5 fl oz vegetable stock
1 sprig of fresh rosemary
chopped fresh parsley and grated orange
    rind, to garnish

GRANDMA'S TIPS

*As a variation, cook the turnips
in a saucepan of boiling water
for 20–25 minutes, or until
tender. Drain well. Place the
juice and grated rind of 1 orange
and 1 tablespoon of honey in the
rinsed-out saucepan and reduce
until thick. Add the cooked
turnips and toss to glaze. This
dish is particularly delicious
served with duck.*

1 Put the turnips into a saucepan of boiling salted water, bring back to the boil and simmer for 10 minutes. Drain well.

2 Melt the butter in the rinsed-out saucepan over a gentle heat, add the turnips and sugar and mix to coat well.

3 Add the stock with the rosemary and bring to the boil. Reduce the heat and simmer for 15–20 minutes with the lid off the pan so that the juices reduce and the turnips are tender and well glazed.

4 Remove the pan from the heat, discard the rosemary and season with salt and pepper to taste.

5 Serve immediately garnished with the chopped parsley and grated orange rind.

ROASTED ROOT VEGETABLES

SERVES 4–6

3 parsnips, cut into 5-cm/2-inch chunks
4 baby turnips, quartered
3 carrots, cut into 5-cm/2-inch chunks
450 g/1 lb butternut squash, peeled and
   cut into 5-cm/2-inch chunks
450 g/1 lb sweet potatoes, peeled and
   cut into 5-cm/2-inch chunks

2 garlic cloves, finely chopped
2 tbsp chopped fresh rosemary
2 tbsp chopped fresh thyme
2 tsp chopped fresh sage
3 tbsp olive oil
salt and pepper
2 tbsp chopped fresh mixed herbs, such
   as parsley, thyme and mint, to garnish

1 Preheat the oven to 220°C/425°F/Gas Mark 7.

2 Arrange all the vegetables in a single layer in a large roasting tin. Scatter over the garlic and the herbs. Pour over the oil and season well with salt and pepper.

3 Toss all the ingredients together until they are well mixed and coated with the oil (you can leave them to marinate at this stage to allow the flavours to be absorbed).

4 Roast the vegetables at the top of the oven for 50–60 minutes until they are cooked and nicely browned. Turn the vegetables over halfway through the cooking time.

5 Serve with a good handful of fresh herbs scattered on top and a final sprinkling of salt and pepper to taste.

HONEYED PARSNIPS

SERVES 4
8 parsnips, peeled and quartered
4 tbsp vegetable oil
1 tbsp honey

GRANDMA'S TIPS
*For a change try substituting
maple syrup for the honey or use
a mixture of root vegetables for
a colourful dish.*

1 Preheat the oven to 180°C/350°F/Gas Mark 4.

2 Bring a large saucepan of water to the boil. Reduce the heat, add the parsnips and cook for 5 minutes. Drain thoroughly.

3 Pour 2 tablespoons of the oil into a shallow, ovenproof dish and add the parsnips. Mix the remaining oil with the honey and drizzle over the parsnips. Roast in the preheated oven for 45 minutes until golden brown and tender. Remove from the oven and serve.

BRUSSELS SPROUTS WITH BUTTERED CHESTNUTS

SERVES 4
350 g/12 oz Brussels sprouts, trimmed
3 tbsp butter
100 g/3½ oz canned whole chestnuts

pinch of nutmeg
salt and pepper
50 g/1¾ oz flaked almonds, to garnish

1 Bring a large saucepan of water to the boil. Add the Brussels sprouts and cook for 5 minutes. Drain thoroughly.

2 Melt the butter in a large saucepan over a medium heat. Add the Brussels sprouts and cook, stirring, for 3 minutes, then add the chestnuts and nutmeg. Season with salt and pepper and stir well. Cook for another 2 minutes, stirring, then remove from the heat. Transfer to a serving dish, scatter over the almonds and serve.

HONEY-GLAZED
RED CABBAGE WITH
SULTANAS

SERVES 4

2 tbsp butter
1 garlic clove, chopped
650 g/1 lb 7 oz red cabbage, shredded

150 g/5½ oz sultanas
1 tbsp honey
100 ml/3½ fl oz red wine
100 ml/3½ fl oz water

1 Melt the butter in a large saucepan over a medium heat. Add the garlic and cook, stirring, for 1 minute, until slightly softened.

2 Add the cabbage and sultanas, then stir in the honey. Cook for another minute. Pour in the wine and water and bring to the boil. Reduce the heat, cover and simmer, stirring occasionally, for about 45 minutes or until the cabbage is cooked. Serve hot.

CHRISTMAS PUDDING

SERVES 4
200 g/7 oz currants
200 g/7 oz raisins
200 g/7 oz sultanas
150 ml/5 fl oz sweet sherry
175 g/6 oz butter, plus extra for greasing
175 g/6 oz brown sugar
4 eggs, beaten
150 g/5½ oz self-raising flour

100 g/3½ oz fresh white or wholemeal
 breadcrumbs
50 g/1¾ oz blanched almonds, chopped
juice of 1 orange
grated rind of ½ orange
grated rind of ½ lemon
½ tsp ground mixed spice
holly leaves, to decorate

GRANDMA'S TIPS
Leftover Christmas pudding makes a lovely dessert when cut into small portions and quickly fried in a little butter. Serve hot with some ice cream.

1 Put the currants, raisins and sultanas into a glass bowl and pour over the sherry. Leave to soak for at least 2 hours.

2 Mix the butter and sugar in a bowl. Beat in the eggs, then fold in the flour. Stir in the soaked fruit and sherry with the breadcrumbs, almonds, orange juice and rind, lemon rind and mixed spice. Grease a pudding basin and press the mixture into it, leaving a gap of 2.5 cm/1 inch at the top. Cut a circle of greaseproof paper 3 cm/1¼ inches larger than the top of the basin, grease with butter and place over the pudding. Secure with string, then top with 2 layers of foil. Place the pudding in a pan filled with boiling water which reaches two-thirds of the way up the basin. Reduce the heat and simmer for 6 hours, topping up with boiling water when necessary.

3 Remove from the heat and leave to cool. Renew the greaseproof paper and foil and refrigerate for 2–8 weeks. To reheat, steam for 2 hours as before. Decorate with holly and serve.

FESTIVE SHERRY TRIFLE

SERVES 8

for the fruit layer
100 g/3½ oz trifle sponges
150 ml/5 fl oz strawberry jam
250 ml/9 fl oz sherry
150 g/5½ oz fresh strawberries, hulled
  and sliced
400 g/14 oz canned mixed fruit, drained
1 large banana, sliced

for the custard layer
6 egg yolks
50 g/1¾ oz caster sugar
500 ml/18 fl oz milk
1 tsp vanilla essence

for the topping
300 ml/10 fl oz double cream
1–2 tbsp caster sugar
chocolate curls or flakes, to decorate

GRANDMA'S TIPS

Instead of trifle sponges, you could use macaroon biscuits, sponge fingers or even sliced Swiss roll. For an even more exotic flavour, try substituting Cassis or Framboise liqueur for the sherry.

1 Spread the trifle sponges with jam, cut them into bite-sized cubes and arrange in the bottom of a large glass serving bowl. Pour over the sherry and leave for 30 minutes.

2 Combine the strawberries, canned fruit and banana and arrange over the sponges. Cover with clingfilm and chill for 30 minutes.

3 To make the custard, put the egg yolks and sugar into a bowl and whisk together. Pour the milk into a pan and warm gently over a low heat. Remove from the heat and gradually stir into the egg mixture, then return the mixture to the pan and stir constantly over a low heat until thickened. Do not boil. Remove from the heat, pour into a bowl and stir in the vanilla. Cool for 1 hour. Spread the custard over the trifle sponge and fruit mixture, cover with clingfilm and chill for 2 hours.

4 To make the topping, whip the cream in a bowl and stir in sugar to taste. Spread over the trifle, then scatter over the chocolate. Cover with clingfilm and refrigerate for at least 2 hours before serving.

FESTIVE MINCE PIES

MAKES 12
200 g/7 oz plain flour, plus extra for
 dusting
100 g/3½ oz butter
25 g/1 oz icing sugar

1 egg yolk
2–3 tbsp milk
300 g/10½ oz mincemeat
1 egg, beaten, for sealing and glazing
icing sugar, for dusting

1 Preheat the oven to 180°C/350°F/Gas Mark 4. Sift the flour into a mixing bowl.
Using your fingertips, rub in the butter until the mixture resembles breadcrumbs. Mix in
the sugar and egg yolk.

2 Stir in enough milk to make a soft dough, turn out onto a lightly floured work surface
and knead lightly until smooth.

3 Shape the dough into a ball and roll out to a thickness of 1 cm/½ inch. Use pastry
cutters to cut out 12 rounds of 7 cm/2¾ inches diameter for the bases and 12 smaller
star shapes for the tops. Dust 12 tartlet tins with flour and line with the dough rounds.
Prick the bases with a fork, then half-fill each pie with mincemeat. Place the star shapes
on top then brush all over with beaten egg. Bake in the preheated oven for 15 minutes.
Remove from the oven and cool on a wire rack. Dust with icing sugar and serve.

SPICED CHRISTMAS PUNCH

SERVES 10
1 litre/1¾ pints of red wine
4 tbsp sugar
1 cinnamon stick
400 ml/14 fl oz boiling water
100 ml/3½ fl oz brandy
100 ml/3½ fl oz sherry

100 ml/3½ fl oz orange liqueur, such as Cointreau
2 seedless oranges, cut into wedges
2 dessert apples, cored and cut into wedges

GRANDMA'S TIPS

You should use heatproof glasses to serve this hot punch. If you are concerned that your glasses may be too fragile, place a metal teaspoon in each glass as you pour so that some of the heat is absorbed by the metal.

1 Put the wine, sugar and cinnamon into a large saucepan and stir together well. Warm over a low heat, stirring, until just starting to simmer, but do not let it boil. Remove from the heat and strain through a sieve. Discard the cinnamon stick.

2 Return the wine to the pan and stir in the water, brandy, sherry and orange liqueur. Add the orange and apple wedges and warm gently over a very low heat, but do not let it boil. Remove from the heat and pour into a large, heatproof punch bowl. Ladle into heatproof glasses and serve hot.

Those with a sweet tooth will fondly remember the delicious aromas of puddings and desserts that would emanate from Grandma's kitchen. Some are really quick and easy to assemble, whilst others take more time, making them best reserved for special occasions and family get-togethers. Chocolate mousse is always popular and, together with profiteroles, banana splits and Black Forest gateau, will give even the most chocoholic cook enough recipes to indulge in. Pies, strudels and crumbles are included to add fruit to the menu — the

GRANDMA'S JUST DESSERTS

fruit can be changed according to taste and season, providing even more diversity. Along with the traditional favourites, such as baked apples, bread and butter pudding and good old rice pudding, you will find recipes for more exotic — but equally well-loved — desserts like Italian tiramisu, Mississippi mud pie and an American-style baked cheesecake. These are dishes that we've grown up with and adopted as our own, despite their far-flung origins. With such a wide selection you are certainly going to be spoilt for choice when it comes to choosing your Grandma's just dessert.

APPLE PIE

SERVES 6
for the pastry
350 g/12 oz plain flour
pinch of salt
85 g/3 oz butter or margarine, cut into
  small pieces
85 g/3 oz lard or white vegetable fat,
  cut into small pieces
about 6 tbsp cold water
beaten egg or milk, for glazing

for the filling
750 g–1 kg/1 lb 10 oz–2 lb 4 oz cooking
  apples, peeled, cored and sliced
125 g/4½ oz caster sugar, plus extra for
  sprinkling
½–1 tsp ground cinnamon, mixed spice
  or ground ginger
1–2 tbsp water (optional)

GRANDMA'S TIPS

When preparing your apples make sure you prepare them one at a time, rather than peeling them all and then slicing them. Place the apple slices in a bowl of water to which has been added the juice of 1 lemon as you go along – this will stop them from discolouring.

1 To make the pastry, sift the flour and salt into a mixing bowl. Add the butter and lard and rub in with your fingertips until the mixture resembles fine breadcrumbs. Add the water and gather the mixture together into a dough. Wrap the dough and chill in the refrigerator for 30 minutes.

2 Preheat the oven to 220°C/425°F/Gas Mark 7. Roll out almost two-thirds of the pastry thinly and use to line a deep 23-cm/9-inch pie plate or pie tin.

3 Mix the apples with the sugar and spice and pack into the pastry case; the filling can come up above the rim. Add the water if needed, particularly if the apples are not very juicy.

4 Roll out the remaining pastry to form a lid. Dampen the edges of the pie rim with water and position the lid, pressing the edges firmly together. Trim and crimp the edges.

5 Use the trimmings to cut out leaves or other shapes to decorate the top of the pie, dampen and attach. Glaze the top of the pie with beaten egg or milk, make 1–2 slits in the top and place the pie on a baking sheet.

6 Bake in the preheated oven for 20 minutes, then reduce the temperature to 180°C/ 350°F/Gas Mark 4 and bake for a further 30 minutes, or until the pastry is a light golden brown. Serve hot or cold, sprinkled with sugar.

LATTICED CHERRY PIE

SERVES 8
for the pastry
140 g/5 oz plain flour, plus extra for
  dusting
¼ tsp baking powder
½ tsp mixed spice
½ tsp salt
50 g/1¾ oz caster sugar
55 g/2 oz cold unsalted butter, diced,
  plus extra for greasing
1 beaten egg, plus extra for glazing
water, for sealing

for the filling
900 g/2 lb stoned fresh cherries, or
  canned cherries, drained
150 g/5½ oz caster sugar
½ tsp almond essence
2 tsp cherry brandy
¼ tsp mixed spice
2 tbsp cornflour
2 tbsp water
25 g/1 oz unsalted butter

freshly whipped cream or ice cream,
  to serve

GRANDMA'S TIPS
*This pie can be made using other
fruits, such as blackberries. To
complement the blackberries,
substitute 2 teaspoons of cassis
liqueur for the cherry brandy.*

1 To make the pastry, sift the flour with the baking powder into a large bowl. Stir in the mixed spice, salt and sugar. Using your fingertips, rub in the butter until the mixture resembles fine breadcrumbs, then make a well in the centre. Pour the beaten egg into the well. Mix with a wooden spoon, then shape the mixture into a dough. Cut the dough in half, and use your hands to roll each half into a ball. Wrap the dough and chill in the refrigerator for 30 minutes.

2 Preheat the oven to 220°C/425°F/Gas Mark 7. Grease a 23-cm/9-inch round pie dish with butter. Roll out the pastry into 2 rounds, each 30 cm/12 inches in diameter. Use one to line the pie dish. Trim the edges, leaving an overhang of 1 cm/½ inch.

3 To make the filling, put half of the cherries and the sugar in a large saucepan. Bring to a simmer over a low heat, stirring, for 5 minutes, or until the sugar has melted. Stir in the almond essence, brandy and mixed spice. In a separate bowl, mix the cornflour and water to form a paste. Remove the saucepan from the heat, stir in the cornflour paste, then return to the heat and stir constantly until the mixture boils and thickens. Leave to cool a little. Stir in the remaining cherries, pour into the pastry case, then dot with butter.

4 Cut the remaining pastry round into long strips 1 cm/½ inch wide. Lay the strips evenly on the top of the filling, crisscrossing to form a lattice. Trim off the ends and seal the edges with water. Use your fingers to crimp around the rim, then brush the top with beaten egg to glaze. Cover with kitchen foil, then bake for 30 minutes. Remove from the oven, discard the foil, then return the pie to the oven for a further 15 minutes, or until cooked and golden. Serve warm with freshly whipped cream or ice cream.

PEAR & PECAN STRUDEL

SERVES 4

2 ripe pears
55 g/2 oz butter
55 g/2 oz fresh white breadcrumbs
55 g/2 oz shelled pecan nuts, chopped
25 g/1 oz light muscovado sugar

finely grated rind of 1 orange
100 g/3½ oz filo pastry, thawed if frozen
6 tbsp orange blossom honey
2 tbsp orange juice
sifted icing sugar, for dusting
Greek-style yogurt, to serve (optional)

1 Preheat the oven to 200°C/400°F/Gas Mark 6. Peel, core and chop the pears. Melt 1 tablespoon of the butter in a frying pan and gently fry the breadcrumbs until golden. Transfer to a bowl and add the pears, nuts, muscovado sugar and orange rind. Put the remaining butter in a small saucepan and heat until melted.

2 Reserve 1 sheet of filo pastry, keeping it well wrapped, and brush the remaining filo sheets with a little melted butter. Spoon some of the nut filling onto the first filo sheet, leaving a 2.5-cm/1-inch margin around the edge. Build up the strudel by placing more buttered filo sheets on top of the first, spreading each one with nut filling as you build up the layers. Drizzle the honey and orange juice over the top.

3 Fold the short ends over the filling, then roll up, starting at a long side. Carefully lift onto a baking sheet, with the join facing up. Brush with any remaining melted butter and crumple the reserved sheet of filo pastry around the strudel. Bake for 25 minutes, or until golden and crisp. Dust with sifted icing sugar and serve warm with Greek-style yogurt, if using.

RHUBARB CRUMBLE

SERVES 6
900 g/2 lb rhubarb
115 g/4 oz caster sugar
grated rind and juice of 1 orange
cream, yogurt or custard, to serve

for the crumble
225 g/8 oz plain or wholemeal flour
115 g/4 oz butter
115 g/4 oz soft brown sugar
1 tsp ground ginger

GRANDMA'S TIPS
Use very young shoots of rhubarb as they are the sweetest. A handful of strawberries would be a good addition as they enhance the flavour and colour. For an added treat, sprinkle over some grated chocolate before adding the crumble toping.

1 Preheat the oven to 190°C/375°F/Gas Mark 5.

2 Cut the rhubarb into 2.5-cm/1-inch lengths and place in a 1.7-litre/3-pint ovenproof dish with the sugar and the orange rind and juice.

3 Make the crumble by placing the flour in a mixing bowl and rubbing in the butter until the mixture resembles breadcrumbs. Stir in the sugar and the ginger.

4 Spread the crumble evenly over the fruit and press down lightly using a fork.

5 Bake in the centre of the oven on a baking tray for 25–30 minutes until the crumble is golden brown.

6 Serve warm with cream, yogurt or custard.

LEMON MERINGUE PIE

SERVES 4
for the pastry
150 g/5½ oz plain flour, plus extra for
    dusting
85 g/3 oz butter, cut into small pieces,
    plus extra for greasing
35 g/1¼ oz icing sugar, sifted
finely grated rind of ½ lemon
½ egg yolk, beaten
1½ tbsp milk

for the filling
3 tbsp cornflour
300 ml/10 fl oz water
juice and grated rind of 2 lemons
175 g/6 oz caster sugar
2 eggs, separated

GRANDMA'S TIPS

This dessert is usually served cold, but why not try it hot? It may sound rather decadent but hot lemon meringue pie with cold ice cream is to die for. Lime or orange juice and rind may be substituted for the lemon juice and rind for a change.

1 To make the pastry, sift the flour into a bowl. Rub in the butter with your fingertips until the mixture resembles fine breadcrumbs. Mix in the remaining ingredients. Knead briefly on a lightly floured work surface. Rest for 30 minutes.

2 Preheat the oven to 180°C/350°F/Gas Mark 4. Grease a 20-cm/8-inch pie dish with butter. Roll out the pastry to a thickness of 5 mm/¼ inch; use it to line the base and sides of the dish. Prick all over with a fork, line with baking paper and fill with baking beans. Bake for 15 minutes. Remove the pastry case from the oven and take out the paper and beans. Reduce the temperature to 150°C/300°F/Gas Mark 2.

3 To make the filling, mix the cornflour with a little of the water. Put the remaining water in a saucepan. Stir in the lemon juice and rind and cornflour paste. Bring to the boil, stirring.

4 Cook for 2 minutes. Cool a little. Stir in 5 tablespoons of the sugar and the egg yolks and pour into the pastry case.

5 Whisk the egg whites in a clean, grease-free bowl until stiff. Gradually whisk in the remaining sugar and spread over the pie. Bake for a further 40 minutes. Remove from oven, cool and serve.

MISSISSIPPI MUD PIE

SERVES 8

for the pastry
225 g/8 oz plain flour, plus extra for
  dusting
2 tbsp cocoa powder
140 g/5 oz butter
2 tbsp caster sugar
1–2 tbsp cold water

for the filling
175 g/6 oz butter
350 g/12 oz soft dark brown sugar

4 eggs, lightly beaten
4 tbsp cocoa powder, sifted
150 g/5½ oz plain chocolate
300 ml/10 fl oz single cream
1 tsp chocolate essence

to decorate
425 ml/15 fl oz double cream, whipped
chocolate flakes and curls

1 To make the pastry, sift the flour and cocoa powder into a mixing bowl. Rub in the butter with your fingertips until the mixture resembles fine breadcrumbs. Stir in the sugar and enough cold water to mix to a soft dough. Wrap the dough and chill in the refrigerator for 15 minutes.

2 Preheat the oven to 190°C/375°F/Gas Mark 5. Roll out the pastry on a lightly floured work surface and use to line a 23-cm/9-inch loose-based flan tin or ceramic flan dish. Line with baking paper and fill with baking beans. Bake in the preheated oven for 15 minutes. Remove the paper and beans from the pastry case and cook for a further 10 minutes until crisp.

3 To make the filling, beat the butter and sugar together in a bowl and gradually beat in the eggs with the cocoa powder. Melt the chocolate and beat it into the mixture with the single cream and the chocolate essence.

4 Reduce the oven temperature to 160°C/325°F/Gas Mark 3. Pour the mixture into the pastry case and bake for 45 minutes, or until the filling has set gently.

5 Let the mud pie cool completely, then transfer the pie to a serving plate, if you like. Cover with the whipped cream.

6 Decorate the pie with chocolate flakes and curls and then chill until ready to serve.

BREAD & BUTTER PUDDING

SERVES 4–6
85 g/3 oz butter, softened
6 slices of thick white bread
55 g/2 oz mixed fruit (sultanas, currants and raisins)
25 g/1 oz candied peel
3 large eggs

300 ml/10 fl oz milk
150 ml/5 fl oz double cream
55 g/2 oz caster sugar
whole nutmeg, for grating
1 tbsp demerara sugar
cream, to serve

GRANDMA'S TIPS

Try using brioche or a lightly fruited loaf instead of the white bread. Any mixture of dried fruits can be used – why not experiment with your favourites? Dried apricots, cherries and cranberries are all nice.

1 Preheat the oven to 180°C/350°F/Gas Mark 4.

2 Use a little of the butter to grease a 20 x 25-cm/8 x 10-inch baking dish and butter the slices of bread. Cut the bread into quarters and arrange half overlapping in the dish.

3 Scatter half the fruit and peel over the bread, cover with the remaining bread slices and add the remaining fruit and peel.

4 In a mixing jug, whisk the eggs well and mix in the milk, cream and sugar. Pour this over the pudding and leave to stand for 15 minutes to allow the bread to soak up some of the egg mixture. Tuck in most of the fruit as you don't want it to burn in the oven. Grate the nutmeg over the top of the pudding, according to taste, and sprinkle over the demerara sugar.

5 Place the pudding on a baking tray and bake at the top of the oven for 30–40 minutes until just set and golden brown.

6 Remove from the oven and serve warm with a little pouring cream.

STICKY TOFFEE
PUDDING

SERVES 4
for the pudding
75 g/2¾ oz sultanas
150 g/5½ oz stoned dates, chopped
1 tsp bicarbonate of soda
2 tbsp butter, plus extra for greasing
200 g/7 oz brown sugar
2 eggs
200 g/7 oz self-raising flour, sifted

for the sticky toffee sauce
2 tbsp butter
175 ml/6 fl oz double cream
200 g/7 oz brown sugar

zested orange rind, to decorate
freshly whipped cream, to serve

GRANDMA'S TIPS
You can make this wicked pudding in individual pudding basins so that everyone has their own portion. Cook for 20–25 minutes and then turn out onto serving plates. This dessert is delicious served with whipped cream, ice cream or clotted cream.

1 To make the pudding, put the sultanas, dates and bicarbonate of soda into a heatproof bowl. Cover with boiling water and leave to soak.

2 Preheat the oven to 180°C/350°F/Gas Mark 4. Grease a round cake tin, 20 cm/ 8 inches in diameter, with butter.

3 Put the remaining butter in a separate bowl, add the sugar and mix well. Beat in the eggs then fold in the flour. Drain the soaked fruits, add to the bowl and mix. Spoon the mixture evenly into the prepared cake tin. Transfer to the preheated oven and bake for 35–40 minutes. The pudding is cooked when a skewer inserted into the centre comes out clean.

4 About 5 minutes before the end of the cooking time, make the sauce. Melt the butter in a saucepan over a medium heat. Stir in the cream and sugar and bring to the boil, stirring constantly. Lower the heat and simmer for 5 minutes.

5 Turn out the pudding onto a serving plate and pour over the sauce. Decorate with zested orange rind and serve with whipped cream.

NEW YORK CHEESECAKE WITH BLUEBERRY COMPOTE

SERVES 8–10
sunflower oil, for brushing
85 g/3 oz unsalted butter
200 g/7 oz digestive biscuits, crushed
450 g/1 lb full-fat cream cheese
100 g/3½ oz caster sugar
2 large eggs
1 large egg yolk
100 ml/3½ fl oz soured cream
1½ tsp vanilla essence

for the topping
400 ml/14 fl oz soured cream
55 g/2 oz caster sugar

for the blueberry compote
55 g/2 oz caster sugar
4 tbsp water
250 g/9 oz fresh blueberries
1 tsp arrowroot

1 Preheat the oven to 150°C/300°F/Gas Mark 2. Brush a 20-cm/8-inch springform cake pan with oil. Melt the butter in a saucepan over a low heat. Stir in the digestive biscuits and press evenly into the base of the pan. Bake for 10 minutes, or until lightly browned, then remove and set aside to cool.

2 Place the cream cheese into a large bowl and beat until smooth. Add the sugar and beat for 1 minute. Add the eggs and egg yolk and beat until well combined. Add the soured cream and vanilla essence and stir until smooth. Pour the mixture into the pan and spread evenly.

3 Bake in the oven for 35–45 minutes or until the edges are firm but the centre is still slightly soft.

4 Remove from the oven and place on a wire rack (still in the pan). Increase the oven temperature to 200°C/400°F/Gas Mark 6.

5 To make the topping, mix together the soured cream and caster sugar, and spread over the top of the cheesecake. Place in the oven and bake for 5–7 minutes until the topping has become very liquid. Turn the oven off but leave the cheesecake inside for 1 hour. Remove from the oven and cool in the pan on a wire rack. Cover and refrigerate overnight.

6 To make the compote, combine the sugar and half the water in a small saucepan and stir over a low heat until the sugar has dissolved. Increase the heat, add the blueberries, then cover and cook for 2–3 minutes or until the blueberries begin to soften. Remove from the heat. Stir together the arrowroot and remaining water in a cup to dissolve the arrowroot. Add to the fruit, return to a low heat, and stir until the juice thickens and turns translucent. Leave to cool completely.

7 Remove the cheesecake from the pan 30 minutes before serving. Spoon the fruit on top and chill until ready to serve.

BLACK FOREST GATEAU

SERVES 8

3 tbsp unsalted butter, melted, plus extra
 for greasing
900 g/2 lb fresh cherries, stoned and
 halved
250 g/9 oz caster sugar
100 ml/3½ fl oz cherry brandy
100 g/3½ oz plain flour

50 g/1¾ oz cocoa powder
½ tsp baking powder
4 eggs
1 litre/1¾ pints double cream

to decorate
grated dark chocolate
whole fresh cherries

GRANDMA'S TIPS

*It is possible to make this
extravagant gateau using canned
cherries – drain the fruit from
the juice and use the liquid to
soak the cake before assembling.
Kirsch or brandy can be used
instead of the cherry brandy.*

1 Preheat the oven to 180°C/350°F/Gas Mark 4. Grease and line a 23-cm/9-inch springform cake pan. Place the cherries in a saucepan, add 3 tablespoons of the sugar and the cherry brandy and bring to a simmer over medium heat. Simmer for 5 minutes. Drain, reserving the syrup. In a large bowl, sift together the flour, cocoa, and baking powder.

2 Place the eggs in a heatproof bowl and beat in 160 g/5¾ oz of the sugar. Place the bowl over a saucepan of simmering water and beat for 6 minutes, or until thickened. Remove from the heat, then gradually fold in the flour mixture and melted butter. Spoon into the cake pan and bake for 40 minutes. Remove from the oven and leave to cool in the pan.

3 Turn out the cake and cut in half horizontally. Mix the double cream and the remaining sugar together and whip lightly until soft peaks form. Spread the reserved syrup over the cut sides of the cake, then spread a layer of whipped cream on the bottom half of the cake, followed by the cherries, and then place the other half on top. Cover the top of the cake with whipped cream, sprinkle over the grated chocolate and decorate with whole fresh cherries.

PROFITEROLES

SERVES 4
for the choux pastry
5 tbsp butter, plus extra for greasing
200 ml/7 fl oz cold water
100 g/3½ oz plain flour
3 eggs, beaten

for the cream filling
300 ml/10 fl oz double cream
3 tbsp caster sugar
1 tsp vanilla essence

for the chocolate & brandy sauce
125 g/4½ oz plain dark chocolate,
   broken into pieces
2½ tbsp butter
6 tbsp water
2 tbsp brandy

GRANDMA'S TIPS

*The choux puffs can be made
two to three days ahead and kept
in an airtight container until
needed. The empty puffs can also
be filled with savoury mixtures,
like prawns and mayonnaise, to
serve with drinks.*

1 Preheat the oven to 200°C/400°F/Gas Mark 6.

2 Grease a large baking sheet with butter. To make the pastry, place the water and butter in a saucepan and bring to the boil. Meanwhile, sift the flour into a bowl. Remove the saucepan from the heat and beat in the flour until smooth. Cool for 5 minutes. Beat in enough of the eggs to give the mixture a soft, dropping consistency. Transfer to a piping bag fitted with a 1-cm/½-inch plain nozzle. Pipe small balls onto the baking sheet. Bake for 25 minutes. Remove from the oven. Pierce each ball with a skewer to let steam escape.

3 To make the filling, whip together the cream, sugar and vanilla essence. Cut the pastry balls almost in half, then fill with the cream filling.

4 To make the sauce, gently melt the chocolate and butter with the water in a small saucepan, stirring, until smooth. Stir in the brandy. Pile the profiteroles into individual serving dishes or into a pyramid on a raised cake stand. Pour over the sauce and serve.

CHOCOLATE MOUSSE

SERVES 4
300 g/10½ oz plain dark chocolate
1½ tbsp unsalted butter
1 tbsp brandy
4 eggs, separated
cocoa powder, for dusting

1 Break the chocolate into small pieces and place in a heatproof bowl set over a pan of simmering water. Add the butter and melt with the chocolate, stirring, until smooth. Remove from the heat, stir in the brandy and leave to cool slightly. Add the egg yolks and beat until smooth.

2 In a separate bowl, whisk the egg whites until stiff peaks have formed, then fold them into the chocolate mixture. Spoon the mixture into 4 small serving bowls and level the surfaces. Transfer to the refrigerator and chill for at least 4 hours until set.

3 Take the mousse out of the refrigerator, dust with cocoa powder and serve.

TRADITIONAL
TIRAMISÙ

SERVES 6

20–24 sponge fingers, about 150 g/5½ oz
2 tbsp cold black coffee
2 tbsp coffee essence
2 tbsp almond liqueur
4 egg yolks
85 g/3 oz caster sugar
a few drops of vanilla essence

grated rind of ½ lemon
350 g/12 oz mascarpone cheese
2 tsp lemon juice
250 ml/9 fl oz double cream
1 tbsp milk
25 g/1 oz lightly toasted flaked almonds
2 tbsp cocoa powder
1 tbsp icing sugar

GRANDMA'S TIPS

This wonderful Italian dessert – a literal translation is 'pick me up' – is very rich and should be served in small portions. A glass of Amaretto is the perfect accompaniment. This dessert looks equally as divine when served in individual ramekins – divide the ingredients accordingly for mouth-watering results.

1 Arrange almost half of the sponge fingers in the base of a serving dish. Place the black coffee, coffee essence and almond liqueur in a bowl and mix. Sprinkle just over half of the mixture over the sponge fingers.

2 Place the egg yolks in a heatproof bowl with the sugar, vanilla essence and lemon rind. Stand the bowl over a saucepan of gently simmering water and whisk until very thick and creamy and the whisk leaves a heavy trail when lifted from the bowl.

3 Place the mascarpone cheese in a separate bowl with the lemon juice and beat until smooth. Stir into the egg mixture and, when evenly blended, pour half of the mixture over the sponge fingers and spread out evenly.

4 Add another layer of sponge fingers, sprinkle with the remaining coffee mixture, then cover with the rest of the cheese and egg mixture. Leave to chill in the refrigerator for at least 2 hours, preferably overnight.

5 Whip the cream and milk together until fairly stiff and spread or pipe over the dessert. Sprinkle with the flaked almonds, then sift an even layer of cocoa powder over the top to cover completely. Finally, sift a layer of icing sugar over the cocoa powder and serve.

BAKED RICE PUDDING

SERVES 4–6
1 tbsp melted unsalted butter
115 g/4 oz pudding rice
55 g/2 oz caster sugar
850 ml/1½ pints full-cream milk
½ tsp vanilla essence

40 g/1½ oz unsalted butter, chilled and cut into pieces
whole nutmeg, for grating
cream, jam, fresh fruit purée, stewed fruit, honey or ice cream, to serve

1 Preheat the oven to 150°C/300°F/Gas Mark 2. Grease a 1.2-litre/2-pint baking dish (a gratin dish is good) with the melted butter, place the rice in the dish and sprinkle with the sugar.

2 Heat the milk in a saucepan until almost boiling, then pour over the rice. Add the vanilla essence and stir well to dissolve the sugar.

3 Cut the butter into small pieces and scatter over the surface of the pudding.

4 Grate the whole nutmeg over the top, using as much as you like to give a good covering.

5 Place the dish on a baking tray and bake in the centre of the oven for 1½–2 hours until the pudding is well browned on the top. You can stir it after the first half hour to disperse the rice.

6 Serve hot topped with cream, jam, fresh fruit purée, stewed fruit, honey or ice cream.

BAKED APPLES

SERVES 4
25 g/1 oz blanched almonds
55 g/2 oz dried apricots
1 piece stem ginger, drained
1 tbsp clear honey

1 tbsp syrup from the stem ginger jar
4 tbsp rolled oats
4 large cooking apples

1 Preheat the oven to 180°C/350°F/Gas Mark 4. Using a sharp knife, chop the almonds very finely. Chop the apricots and stem ginger very finely. Reserve.

2 Place the honey and syrup in a saucepan and heat until the honey has melted. Stir in the oats and cook gently over a low heat for 2 minutes. Remove the saucepan from the heat and stir in the almonds, apricots and stem ginger.

3 Core the apples, widen the tops slightly and score around the circumference of each to prevent the skins bursting during cooking. Place them in an ovenproof dish and fill the cavities with the stuffing. Pour just enough water into the dish to come about one-third of the way up the apples. Bake in the preheated oven for 40 minutes, or until tender. Serve immediately.

BLUEBERRY PANCAKES

MAKES 10–12
140 g/5 oz plain flour
2 tbsp caster sugar
2 tbsp baking powder
½ tsp salt
225 ml/8 fl oz buttermilk
3 tbsp butter, melted

1 large egg
140 g/5 oz fresh blueberries, plus
  extra to serve
sunflower oil, for oiling
butter and warmed maple syrup,
  to serve

GRANDMA'S TIPS

These small pancakes are ideal to serve for breakfast with crispy bacon or scrambled eggs and any other accompaniment of your choice.

1 Preheat the oven to 140°C/275°F/Gas Mark 1. Sieve the flour, sugar, baking powder and salt together into a large bowl and make a well in the centre.

2 Beat the buttermilk, butter and egg together in a separate small bowl, then pour the mixture into the well in the dry ingredients. Beat the dry ingredients into the liquid, gradually drawing them in from the side, until a smooth batter is formed. Gently stir in the blueberries.

3 Heat a large frying pan over a medium-high heat until a splash of water dances on the surface. Using a pastry brush or crumpled piece of kitchen paper, oil the base of the frying pan.

4 Drop about 4 tablespoons of batter separately into the frying pan and spread each out into a 10-cm/4-inch round. Continue adding as many pancakes as will fit in your frying pan. Cook until small bubbles appear on the surface, then flip over with a spatula or palette knife and cook the pancakes on the other side for a further 1–2 minutes until golden brown.

5 Transfer the pancakes to a warmed plate and keep warm in the preheated oven while you cook the remaining batter, lightly oiling the frying pan as before. Make a stack of the pancakes with baking paper in between each pancake.

6 Serve with a knob of butter on top of each pancake and warm maple syrup for pouring over.

BANANA SPLITS

SERVES 4
4 bananas
6 tbsp chopped mixed nuts, to serve

for the vanilla ice cream
300 ml/10 fl oz milk
1 tsp vanilla essence
3 egg yolks
100 g/3½ oz caster sugar
300 ml/10 fl oz double cream, whipped

for the chocolate rum sauce
125 g/4½ oz plain chocolate, broken into
   small pieces
2½ tbsp butter
6 tbsp water
1 tbsp rum

GRANDMA'S TIPS

For a quick and easy pudding, use shop-bought ice cream. If you're serving the banana splits to children, omit the rum from the chocolate sauce.

1 To make the ice cream, heat the milk and vanilla essence in a saucepan until almost boiling. In a bowl, beat together the egg yolks and sugar. Remove the milk from the heat and stir a little into the egg mixture. Transfer the mixture to the pan. Stir over a low heat until thick. Do not boil. Remove from the heat. Cool for 30 minutes, fold in the cream, cover with clingfilm and chill for 1 hour. Transfer into an ice-cream maker and process for 15 minutes. Alternatively, transfer into a freezerproof container and freeze for 1 hour, then place in a bowl and beat to break up the ice crystals. Put back in the container and freeze for 30 minutes. Repeat twice more, freezing for 30 minutes and whisking each time.

2 To make the sauce, melt the chocolate and butter with the water in a saucepan, stirring. Remove from the heat and stir in the rum. Peel the bananas, slice lengthways and arrange on 4 serving dishes. Top with ice cream and nuts and serve with the sauce.

Remember the smells of home-baked cakes, biscuits and scones when
you were young? It was on those days that you learned to rub fat
into flour with your fingertips to make pastry and to beat sugar
and butter together to make cakes. It was fun to sprinkle flour over
the kitchen table, roll out biscuit dough and cut it into different
shapes — Grandma didn't seem to mind the mess. The best bit was
eating the misshapen bits when they were still hot from the oven.
This chapter provides recipes for all kinds of delicious goodies — from

GRANDMA'S BAKING DAY

a classic Victoria sponge cake to indulgent chocolate brownies.
Perhaps it will even encourage you to bake with your own children
or grandchildren — they will particularly enjoy helping to make the
easy nutty flapjacks or assembling the lemon butterfly cakes. All of
the recipes in this section are perfect for filling those little gaps in
the day, be it mid-morning or tea-time — but make sure you put
the rest away in an airtight tin so that there is always something
delicious to hand when friends or family come by.

SANDWICH CAKE WITH CHOCOLATE TOPPING

SERVES 8–10
for the cakes
125 g/4½ oz soft margarine, plus extra
for greasing
125 g/4½ oz caster sugar
2 eggs
1 tbsp golden syrup
125 g/4½ oz self-raising flour, sifted
2 tbsp cocoa powder, sifted

for the filling and topping
50 g/1¾ oz icing sugar, sifted
25 g/1 oz butter
100 g/3½ oz milk chocolate
a little white chocolate, melted
(optional)

GRANDMA'S TIPS

This simple chocolate-flavoured Victoria sandwich cake is a good base for all sorts of desserts. It is ideal as a birthday cake to decorate as you wish, or to serve with raspberries and cream for a summer dessert.

1 Preheat the oven to 160°C/325°F/Gas Mark 3. Lightly grease two 18-cm/7-inch shallow cake tins.

2 Place all of the ingredients for the cake in a large mixing bowl and beat with a wooden spoon or electric hand whisk to form a smooth mixture.

3 Divide the mixture between the prepared tins and level the tops. Bake in the preheated oven for 20 minutes, or until springy to the touch. Cool for a few minutes in the tins before transferring to a wire rack to cool completely.

4 To make the filling, beat the icing sugar and butter together in a bowl until light and fluffy. Melt the milk chocolate and beat half into the filling mixture. Use the filling to sandwich the 2 cakes together.

5 Spread the remaining melted milk chocolate over the top of the cake. Pipe circles of contrasting melted white chocolate and feather into the milk chocolate with a cocktail stick, if liked. Leave to set before serving.

VICTORIA SPONGE CAKE

SERVES 8–10

175 g/6 oz butter, at room temperature,
 plus extra for greasing
175 g/6 oz caster sugar
3 eggs, beaten

175 g/6 oz self-raising flour
pinch of salt
3 tbsp raspberry jam
1 tbsp caster or icing sugar

GRANDMA'S TIPS

These cakes can also be flavoured with grated lemon rind and sandwiched together with lemon curd for a summery feel. For a simple butter cream filling, beat together equal quantities of butter and icing sugar until light and fluffy.

1 Preheat the oven to 180°C/350°F/Gas Mark 4.

2 Grease two 20-cm/8-inch sponge tins and line with greaseproof paper or baking paper.

3 Cream the butter and sugar together in a mixing bowl using a wooden spoon or a hand-held mixer until the mixture is pale in colour and light and fluffy.

4 Add the egg a little at a time, beating well after each addition.

5 Sift the flour and salt and carefully add to the mixture, folding it in with a metal spoon or a spatula.

6 Divide the mixture between the tins and smooth over with the spatula.

7 Place them on the same shelf in the centre of the oven and bake for 25–30 minutes until well risen, golden brown and beginning to shrink from the sides of the tin.

8 Remove from the oven and allow to stand for 1 minute.

9 Loosen the cakes from around the edge of the tins using a palette knife. Turn the cakes out onto a clean tea towel, remove the paper and invert them onto a wire rack (this prevents the wire rack from marking the top of the cakes).

10 When completely cool, sandwich together with the jam and sprinkle with the sugar. The cake is delicious when freshly baked, but any remaining cake can be stored in an airtight tin for up to 1 week.

LEMON DRIZZLE CAKE

SERVES 8
butter, for greasing
200 g/7 oz plain flour
2 tsp baking powder
200 g/7 oz caster sugar
4 eggs
150 ml/5 fl oz soured cream
grated rind of 1 large lemon
4 tbsp lemon juice
150 ml/5 fl oz sunflower oil

for the syrup
4 tbsp icing sugar
3 tbsp lemon juice

1 Preheat the oven to 180°C/350°F/Gas Mark 4. Lightly grease a 20-cm/8-inch loose-bottom round cake tin and line the base with baking paper.

2 Sieve the flour and baking powder into a mixing bowl and stir in the caster sugar.

3 In a separate bowl, whisk the eggs, soured cream, lemon rind, lemon juice and oil together.

4 Pour the egg mixture into the dry ingredients and mix well until evenly combined.

5 Pour the mixture into the prepared tin and bake in the preheated oven for 45–60 minutes until risen and golden brown.

6 Meanwhile, to make the syrup, mix together the icing sugar and lemon juice in a small saucepan. Stir over a low heat until just beginning to bubble and turn syrupy.

7 As soon as the cake comes out of the oven, prick the surface with a fine skewer, then brush the syrup over the top. Leave the cake to cool completely in the tin before turning out and serving.

RICH FRUIT CAKE

SERVES 12
butter, for greasing
175 g/6 oz stoned unsweetened dates
125 g/4½ oz ready-to-eat dried prunes
200 ml/7 fl oz unsweetened orange juice
2 tbsp black treacle
1 tsp finely grated lemon rind
1 tsp finely grated orange rind
225 g/8 oz wholemeal self-raising flour
1 tsp mixed spice
125 g/4½ oz seedless raisins

125 g/4½ oz sultanas
125 g/4½ oz currants
125 g/4½ oz dried cranberries
3 large eggs, separated

to decorate
1 tbsp apricot jam, warmed
icing sugar, for dusting
175 g/6 oz sugar paste
strips of orange rind
strips of lemon rind

GRANDMA'S TIPS

This healthy take on the typically rich fruit cake would make an ideal Christmas or celebration cake. It keeps well in an airtight tin and can be covered with marzipan and royal icing and decorated with Christmas figures or flowers.

1 Grease and line a deep 20-cm/8-inch round cake tin. Chop the dates and prunes and place in a large, heavy-based saucepan. Pour over the orange juice and simmer for 10 minutes. Remove the saucepan from the heat and beat the fruit mixture until puréed. Add the treacle and citrus rinds and leave to cool.

2 Preheat the oven to 160°C/325°F/Gas Mark 3. Sift the flour and mixed spice into a bowl, adding any bran that remains in the sieve. Add the raisins, sultanas, currants and dried cranberries. When the date and prune mixture is cool, whisk in the egg yolks. Whisk the egg whites in a clean bowl until stiff. Spoon the fruit mixture into the dry ingredients and mix together. Gently fold in the egg whites. Transfer to the prepared tin and bake in the preheated oven for 1½ hours. Leave to cool in the tin.

3 Remove the cake from the tin and brush the top with jam. Dust the work surface with icing sugar and roll out the sugar paste thinly. Lay the sugar paste over the top of the cake and trim the edges. Decorate with orange and lemon rind.

CLASSIC CARROT CAKE

SERVES 12
butter, for greasing
125 g/4½ oz self-raising flour
pinch of salt
1 tsp ground cinnamon
125 g/4½ oz soft brown sugar
2 eggs
100 ml/3½ fl oz sunflower oil
125 g/4½ oz carrot, peeled and
  finely grated
25 g/1 oz desiccated coconut
25 g/1 oz walnuts, chopped
walnut pieces, to decorate

for the icing
50 g/1¾ oz butter, softened
50 g/1¾ oz soft cheese
225 g/8 oz icing sugar, sifted
1 tsp lemon juice

GRANDMA'S TIPS
This cake freezes well (without the icing) and can be kept for up to three months. It's perfect for a teatime treat as well as a quick dessert served with some ice cream.

1 Preheat the oven to 180°C/350°F/Gas Mark 4. Lightly grease a 20-cm/8-inch square cake tin and line the base with baking paper.

2 Sift the flour, salt and ground cinnamon into a large bowl and stir in the brown sugar. Add the eggs and oil to the dry ingredients and mix well.

3 Stir in the grated carrot, desiccated coconut and chopped walnuts.

4 Pour the mixture into the prepared tin and bake in the preheated oven for 20–25 minutes, or until just firm to the touch. Leave to cool in the tin.

5 Meanwhile, make the icing. In a bowl, beat together the butter, soft cheese, icing sugar and lemon juice until the mixture is fluffy and creamy.

6 Turn the cake out of the tin and cut into 12 bars or slices. Spread with the icing and then decorate with walnut pieces.

APPLE STREUSEL CAKE

SERVES 8
115 g/4 oz butter, plus extra for greasing
450 g/1 lb cooking apples
175 g/6 oz self-raising flour
1 tsp ground cinnamon
pinch of salt
115 g/4 oz caster sugar
2 eggs

1–2 tbsp milk
icing sugar, for dusting

for the streusel topping
115 g/4 oz self-raising flour
85 g/3 oz butter
85 g/3 oz caster sugar

1 Preheat the oven to 180°C/350°F/Gas Mark 4, then grease a 23-cm/9-inch springform cake tin. To make the streusel topping, sift the flour into a bowl and rub in the butter until the mixture resembles coarse crumbs. Stir in the sugar and reserve.

2 Peel, core and thinly slice the apples. To make the cake, sift the flour into a bowl with the cinnamon and salt. Place the butter and sugar in a separate bowl and beat together until light and fluffy. Gradually beat in the eggs, adding a little of the flour mixture with the last addition of egg. Gently fold in half the remaining flour mixture, then fold in the rest with the milk.

3 Spoon the mixture into the prepared tin and smooth the top. Cover with the sliced apples and sprinkle the streusel topping evenly over the top. Bake in the preheated oven for 1 hour, or until browned and firm to the touch. Leave to cool in the tin before opening the sides. Dust the cake with icing sugar before serving.

COFFEE &
WALNUT CAKE

SERVES 8

for the icing
6 tbsp cocoa powder
2 tbsp cornflour
6 tbsp caster sugar
125 ml/4 fl oz strong black coffee,
    cooled
250 ml/9 fl oz milk

walnut halves, to decorate

for the sponge
85 g/3 oz butter, softened, plus extra for
    greasing
275 g/9½ oz plain flour
1 tbsp baking powder
85 g/3 oz caster sugar
2 eggs
150 ml/5 fl oz milk
3 tbsp hot strong black coffee
60 g/2¼ oz shelled walnuts, chopped
50 g/1¾ oz sultanas

GRANDMA'S TIPS

This soft-textured cake is always very popular. The chocolate topping can be replaced with a simple sugar icing (made with icing sugar and water) if preferred.

1 To make the icing, put all the ingredients into a food processor and process until creamy. Transfer to a saucepan and heat, stirring, over a medium heat until bubbling. Cook for 1 minute, then pour into a heatproof bowl. Leave to cool, then cover with clingfilm and refrigerate for at least 2 hours.

2 Preheat the oven to 190°C/375°F/Gas Mark 5. Grease a 23-cm/9-inch loose-bottomed cake tin with butter and line with baking paper. To make the sponge, sift the flour and baking powder into a bowl, then stir in the sugar. In a separate bowl, beat together the butter, eggs, milk and coffee, then mix into the flour mixture.

3 Stir in the chopped walnuts and the sultanas. Spoon the mixture into the prepared cake tin and level the surface. Transfer to the preheated oven and bake for 1 hour. Remove from the oven and leave to cool. When cool enough to handle, turn out on to a wire rack and leave to cool completely. Spread the icing over the top of the cooled cake, decorate with the walnut halves and serve.

GINGERBREAD

MAKES 12–16
450 g/1 lb plain flour
3 tsp baking powder
1 tsp bicarbonate of soda
3 tsp ground ginger
175 g/6 oz unsalted butter
175 g/6 oz soft brown sugar

175 g/6 oz black treacle
175 g/6 oz golden syrup
1 egg, beaten
300 ml/10 fl oz milk
cream or warmed golden syrup,
  to serve

1 Line a 23-cm/9-inch square cake tin, 5 cm/2 inches deep, with greaseproof or baking paper.

2 Preheat the oven to 160ºC/325ºF/Gas Mark 3.

3 Sift the flour, baking powder, bicarbonate of soda and ground ginger into a large mixing bowl.

4 Place the butter, sugar, treacle and syrup in a medium saucepan and heat over a low heat until the butter has melted and the sugar dissolved. Allow to cool a little.

5 Mix the beaten egg with the milk and add to the cooled syrup mixture.

6 Add all the liquid ingredients to the flour mixture and beat well using a wooden spoon until the mixture is smooth and glossy.

7 Pour the mixture into the prepared tin and bake in the centre of the oven for 1½ hours until well risen and just firm to the touch. This gives a lovely sticky gingerbread, but if you like a firmer cake cook for a further 15 minutes.

8 Remove from the oven and allow the cake to cool in the tin. When cool, remove the cake from the tin with the lining paper. Over wrap with foil and place in an airtight tin for up to 1 week to allow the flavours to mature.

9 Cut into wedges and serve cold with tea or coffee or warm with cream and golden syrup.

MARBLED CHOCOLATE &
ORANGE TEABREAD

SERVES 12

150 g/5½ oz butter, softened, plus extra
   for greasing
75 g/2¾ oz plain chocolate, broken
   into pieces
250 g/9 oz caster sugar

5 large eggs, beaten
150 g/5½ oz plain flour
2 tsp baking powder
pinch of salt
grated rind of 2 oranges

1 Preheat the oven to 180°C/350°F/Gas Mark 4. Grease and line the base and ends of two 450-g/1-lb loaf tins. Place the chocolate in a heatproof bowl set over a saucepan of simmering water, making sure that the base of the bowl does not touch the water. Remove from the heat once the chocolate has melted.

2 Place the butter and sugar in a separate bowl and beat until light and fluffy. Gradually beat in the eggs. Sift the flour, baking powder and salt into the mixture and fold in.

3 Transfer one-third of the mixture to the melted chocolate and stir together. Stir the orange rind into the remaining mixture and place one-quarter of the mixture in each cake tin, spread in an even layer.

4 Drop spoonfuls of the chocolate mixture on top, dividing it between the 2 tins, but do not smooth it out. Divide the remaining orange mixture between the 2 tins, then, using a knife, gently swirl the top 2 layers together to give a marbled effect. Bake in the preheated oven for 35–40 minutes, or until a skewer inserted into the centre comes out clean.

5 Leave to cool in the tins for 10 minutes, then turn out, peel off the lining paper and transfer to a wire rack to cool completely.

BANANA LOAF

SERVES 6
unsalted butter, for greasing
125 g/4½ oz white self-raising flour
100 g/3½ oz light brown self-raising flour
150 g/5½ oz demerara sugar
pinch of salt
½ tsp ground cinnamon

½ tsp ground nutmeg
2 large ripe bananas, peeled
175 ml/6 fl oz orange juice
2 eggs, beaten
4 tbsp rapeseed oil
honey, to serve

GRANDMA'S TIPS
This loaf is delicious simply buttered or served with chopped banana, walnuts and a drizzle of honey. Try toasting a slice or two the next day to bring out even more of the banana flavour.

1 Preheat the oven to 180°C/350°F/Gas Mark 4. Lightly grease and line a 450-g/1-lb loaf tin.

2 Sift the flours, sugar, a pinch of salt, and the spices into a large bowl.

3 In a separate bowl, mash the bananas with the orange juice, then stir in the eggs and oil. Pour into the dry ingredients and mix well.

4 Spoon into the prepared loaf tin and bake in the preheated oven for 1 hour, then test to see if it is cooked by inserting a skewer into the centre. If it comes out clean, the loaf is done. If not, bake for a further 10 minutes and test again.

5 Remove from the oven and leave to cool in the tin. Turn the loaf out, slice and serve with honey.

STRAWBERRY ROULADE

SERVES 8
3 large eggs
125 g/4½ oz caster sugar
125 g/4½ oz plain flour
1 tbsp hot water

for the filling
200 ml/7 fl oz low-fat fromage frais
1 tsp almond essence
225 g/8 oz small strawberries
15 g/½ oz flaked almonds, toasted
icing sugar, for dusting

GRANDMA'S TIPS

Making a roulade looks quite difficult, but it really is quite simple when you use baking paper. Try varying the filling by using raspberries instead of the strawberries or whipped cream instead of the mascarpone. For a simple roulade, fill with jam – this makes a good base for a trifle.

1 Preheat the oven to 220°C/425°F/Gas Mark 7. Line a 35 x 25-cm/14 x 10-inch Swiss roll tin with baking paper. Place the eggs in a large, heatproof bowl with the caster sugar, place over a saucepan of hot water and, using an electric beater, beat until pale and thick.

2 Remove the bowl from the saucepan. Sift in the flour and fold into the eggs with the hot water. Pour the mixture into the prepared tin and bake in the preheated oven for 8–10 minutes, or until golden and set.

3 Transfer the sponge to a sheet of baking paper. Peel off the lining paper and roll up the sponge tightly along with the baking paper. Wrap in a tea towel and cool until completely cooled.

4 Mix the fromage frais and almond essence together in a bowl. Leave the mixture to chill in the refrigerator until required. Wash, hull and slice the strawberries.

5 Unroll the sponge, spread the fromage frais mixture over the sponge and sprinkle with the sliced strawberries. Roll the sponge up again and transfer to a serving plate. Sprinkle with almonds, lightly dust with icing sugar and serve.

CHOCOLATE CHIP
BROWNIES

MAKES 12

225 g/8 oz butter, softened, plus extra
   for greasing
150 g/5½ oz plain chocolate, broken into
   pieces
225 g/8 oz self-raising flour

125 g/4½ oz caster sugar
4 eggs, beaten
75 g/2¾ oz pistachio nuts, chopped
100 g/3½ oz white chocolate, roughly
   chopped
icing sugar, for dusting

1 Preheat the oven to 180°C/350°F/Gas Mark 4. Grease a 23-cm/9-inch square baking tin and line with baking paper.

2 Place the chocolate and softened butter in a heatproof bowl set over a saucepan of simmering water. Stir until melted, then leave to cool slightly.

3 Sift the flour into a separate bowl and stir in the caster sugar.

4 Stir the beaten eggs into the chocolate mixture, then pour the mixture into the flour and sugar and beat well. Stir in the pistachio nuts and white chocolate, then pour the mixture into the tin, using a palette knife to spread it evenly.

5 Bake in the preheated oven for 30–35 minutes, or until firm to the touch around the edges. Leave to cool in the tin for 20 minutes. Turn out onto a wire rack. Dust with icing sugar and leave to cool completely. Cut into 12 pieces and serve.

NUTTY FLAPJACKS

MAKES 16
115 g/4 oz butter, plus extra for greasing
200 g/7 oz rolled oats
115 g/4 oz chopped hazelnuts

55 g/2 oz plain flour
2 tbsp golden syrup
85 g/3 oz light muscovado sugar

GRANDMA'S TIPS

These are very handy for lunch boxes or to take along on a picnic. Honey can be used instead of golden syrup and some dried fruit, such as apricots or cranberries, can be added for colour and flavour.

1 Preheat the oven to 180°C/350°F/Gas Mark 4, then grease a 23-cm/9-inch square ovenproof dish or cake tin. Place the rolled oats, chopped hazelnuts and flour in a large mixing bowl and stir together.

2 Place the butter, syrup and sugar in a saucepan over a low heat and stir until melted. Pour onto the dry ingredients and mix well. Turn the mixture into the prepared ovenproof dish and smooth the surface with the back of a spoon.

3 Bake in the oven for 20–25 minutes, or until golden and firm to the touch. Mark into 16 pieces and leave to cool in the tin. When completely cooled, cut through with a sharp knife and remove from the tin.

LEMON BUTTERFLY CAKES

MAKES 12
115 g/4 oz self-raising flour
½ tsp baking powder
115 g/4 oz butter, softened
115 g/4 oz caster sugar
2 eggs, beaten
finely grated rind of ½ lemon

2–4 tbsp milk
icing sugar, for dusting

for the filling
55 g/2 oz butter
115 g/4 oz icing sugar
1 tbsp lemon juice

GRANDMA'S TIPS

Cupcakes are always a favourite for children's parties. You can use multi-coloured paper cases to make them look even more attractive. A whole strawberry, raspberry or glacé cherry can be popped on top to decorate.

1 Preheat the oven to 190°C/375°F/Gas Mark 5. Place 12 paper cases in a bun tin. Sift the flour and baking powder into a bowl. Add the butter, sugar, eggs, lemon rind and enough milk to give a medium-soft consistency. Beat the mixture thoroughly until smooth, then divide among the paper cases and bake in the preheated oven for 15–20 minutes, or until well risen and golden. Transfer to wire racks to cool.

2 To make the filling, place the butter in a bowl. Sift in the icing sugar and add the lemon juice. Beat well until smooth and creamy. When the cakes are completely cooled, use a sharp-pointed vegetable knife to cut a circle from the top of each cake, then cut each circle in half.

3 Spoon a little buttercream into the centre of each cake and press the 2 semi-circular pieces into it to resemble wings. Dust the cakes with sifted icing sugar before serving.

BLUEBERRY MUFFINS

MAKES 10–12
250 g/9 oz plain white flour
1 tsp baking powder
pinch of salt
100 g/3½ oz demerara sugar, plus
  1 tbsp for sprinkling

1 egg, beaten
225 ml/8 fl oz milk
55 g/2 oz unsalted butter, melted
125 g/4½ oz small fresh blueberries

1 Preheat the oven to 180°C/350°F/Gas Mark 4. Line a 12-hole muffin tin with paper cases. Sift the flour, baking powder and salt into a large bowl and stir in the sugar.

2 Add the beaten egg, milk and melted butter to the dry ingredients and stir in lightly until just combined – do not overmix. Carefully fold in the blueberries.

3 Spoon the mixture into the paper cases, taking care not to overfill, and sprinkle with the remaining sugar.

4 Bake in the preheated oven for 25–30 minutes until golden brown and firm. Transfer to a wire rack to cool a little.

SCONES

MAKES 10–12
450 g/1 lb plain flour, plus extra
   for dusting
½ tsp salt
2 tsp baking powder
55 g/2 oz butter

2 tbsp caster sugar
250 ml/9 fl oz milk
3 tbsp milk, for glazing
strawberry jam and clotted cream,
   to serve

GRANDMA'S TIPS

*These delicious scones are at their
best straight from the oven. You
can also add 55 g/2 oz dried
mixed fruit to the mixture. For
savoury scones to serve with soup,
add 55 g/2 oz grated cheese to
the mix and omit the sugar.*

1 Preheat the oven to 220°C/425°F/Gas Mark 7.

2 Sift the flour, salt and baking powder into a bowl. Rub in the butter until the mixture resembles breadcrumbs. Stir in the sugar.

3 Make a well in the centre and pour in the milk. Stir in using a palette knife and make a soft dough.

4 Turn the mixture onto a floured surface and lightly flatten the dough until it is of an even thickness, about 1 cm/½ inch. Don't be heavy-handed, scones need a light touch.

5 Use a 6-cm/2½-inch pastry cutter to cut out the scones and place on the baking tray.

6 Glaze with a little milk and bake for 10–12 minutes, until golden and well risen.

7 Cool on a wire rack and serve freshly baked with strawberry jam and clotted cream.

SHORTBREAD

MAKES 8
115 g/4 oz butter, cut into small pieces, plus extra for greasing
175 g/6 oz plain flour, plus extra for dusting

pinch of salt
55 g/2 oz caster sugar, plus extra for dusting

GRANDMA'S TIPS

To give shortbread a bit more texture, replace 55 g/ 2 oz of the flour with semolina, which will give it a more granular, slightly gritty texture.

1 Preheat the oven to 150°C/300°F/Gas Mark 2.

2 Grease a 20-cm/8-inch fluted cake tin or flan tin.

3 Mix together the flour, salt and sugar. Rub the butter into the dry ingredients. Continue to work the mixture until it forms a soft dough. Make sure you do not overwork the shortbread or it will be tough, not crumbly as it should be.

4 Lightly press the dough into the cake tin. If you don't have a fluted tin, roll out the dough on a lightly floured board, place on a baking tray and pinch the edges to form a scalloped pattern.

5 Mark into 8 pieces with a knife. Prick all over with a fork and bake in the centre of the oven for 45–50 minutes until the shortbread is firm and just coloured.

6 Allow to cool in the tin and dust with the sugar. Cut into portions and remove to a wire rack. Store in an airtight container in a cool place until needed.

CHOCOLATE CHIP
COOKIES

MAKES 18

125 g/4½ oz soft margarine, plus extra
  for greasing
175 g/6 oz plain flour
1 tsp baking powder

85 g/3 oz light muscovado sugar
5 tbsp caster sugar
½ tsp vanilla essence
1 egg
125 g/4½ oz dark chocolate chips

1 Preheat the oven to 190°C/375°F/Gas Mark 5. Lightly grease two baking trays.

2 Place all of the ingredients in a large mixing bowl and beat until well combined.

3 Place tablespoonfuls of the mixture onto the baking trays, spacing them well apart to allow for spreading during cooking.

4 Bake in the preheated oven for 10–12 minutes or until the cookies are golden brown.

5 Using a palette knife, transfer the cookies to a wire rack to cool completely before serving.

ORANGE GINGERNUTS

MAKES 30
125 g/4½ oz butter, plus extra for
  greasing
350 g/12 oz self-raising flour
pinch of salt
200 g/7 oz caster sugar

I tbsp ground ginger
I tsp bicarbonate of soda
75 g/2¾ oz golden syrup
I egg, beaten
I tsp grated orange rind

GRANDMA'S TIPS
You may find it easier to roll out the dough into a log shape and then cut into slices before placing the gingernuts on the baking trays.

1 Preheat the oven to 160°C/325°F/Gas Mark 3. Lightly grease several baking trays.

2 Sieve the flour, salt, sugar, ginger and bicarbonate of soda into a large mixing bowl.

3 Heat the butter and golden syrup together in a saucepan over a very low heat until the butter has melted.

4 Leave the butter mixture to cool slightly, then pour it onto the dry ingredients.

5 Add the egg and orange rind and mix thoroughly.

6 Using your hands, carefully shape the dough into 30 even-sized balls.

7 Place the balls well apart on the prepared baking trays, then flatten them slightly with your fingers.

8 Bake in the preheated oven for 15–20 minutes, then transfer them to a wire rack to cool.

CLASSIC OATMEAL COOKIES

MAKES 30
175 g/6 oz butter or margarine, plus
    extra for greasing
275 g/9½ oz demerara sugar
I egg
4 tbsp water

I tsp vanilla essence
375 g/13 oz rolled oats
140 g/5 oz plain flour
I tsp salt
½ tsp bicarbonate of soda

GRANDMA'S TIPS

*After you've made these classic
cookies once, why not vary
them by substituting desiccated
coconut for some of the oats?
You could also add some chopped
nuts, chopped glacé cherries or
chocolate chips.*

1 Preheat the oven to 350°F/180°C/Gas Mark 4 and grease a large baking sheet.

2 Cream the butter and sugar together in a large mixing bowl. Beat in the egg, water and vanilla essence until the mixture is smooth.

3 In a separate bowl, mix the oats, flour, salt and bicarbonate of soda. Gradually stir the oat mixture into the butter mixture until thoroughly combined.

4 Put 30 rounded tablespoonfuls of cookie mixture onto the greased baking sheet, making sure they are well spaced. Transfer to the preheated oven and bake for 15 minutes, or until the cookies are golden brown.

5 Remove the cookies from the oven and place on a wire rack to cool before serving.

WHITE BREAD

MAKES 1 LARGE LOAF
450 g/1 lb strong white flour, plus 2 tbsp
   for dusting
1 tsp salt

7 g/¼ oz easy-blend dried yeast
1 tbsp vegetable oil or melted butter,
   plus 1 tsp for greasing
300 ml/10 fl oz warm water

1 Mix the flour, salt and yeast together in a mixing bowl. Add the oil and water and stir well to form a soft dough.

2 Turn the dough out onto a lightly floured board and knead well by hand for 5–7 minutes. Alternatively, use a free-standing electric mixer for this and knead the dough with the dough hook for 4–5 minutes. The dough should have a smooth appearance and feel elastic.

3 Return the dough to the bowl, cover with clingfilm and leave to rise in a warm place for 1 hour. When it has doubled in size, turn it out onto a floured board and knead again for 30 seconds; this is known as 'knocking back'. Knead it until smooth.

4 Shape the dough into a rectangle the length of the tin and three times the width. Grease the tin well, fold the dough into three lengthways and put it in the tin with the join underneath for a well-shaped loaf. Cover and leave to rise in a warm place for 30 minutes until it has risen well above the tin.

5 Preheat the oven to 220°C/425°F/Gas Mark 7. Bake in the centre of the preheated oven for 25–30 minutes until firm and golden brown. Test that the loaf is cooked by tapping it on the bottom – it should sound hollow. Cool on a cooling rack for 30 minutes. Store in an airtight container in a cool place for 3–4 days.

Index